Illusion and spontaneity in psychoanalysis

ILLUSION AND SPONTANEITY IN PSYCHOANALYSIS

John Klauber and others

'. . . an association in which the free development of each is the condition of the free development of all'

Free Association Books / London / 1987

First published in Great Britain 1987 by
Free Association Books
26 Freegrove Road
London N7 9RQ

By arrangement with Mark Paterson

British Library Cataloguing in Publication Data
Klauber, John
  Illusion and spontaneity in psychoanalysis
  1. Psychoanalysis
  I. Title
  150.19'5   BF173

  ISBN 0 946960 76 3 Hbk
  ISBN 0 946960 77 1 Pbk

Typeset by Input Typesetting Ltd, London

Printed and bound in Great Britain by
Short Run Press, Exeter

For Jane and Susie

CONTENTS

ACKNOWLEDGEMENTS

The publishers and Ruth Brook Klauber are very grateful to Jill Duncan, Librarian at the Institute of Psycho-Analysis, London for completing the references within John Klauber's lectures.

Acknowledgement is also due to Springer-Verlag Berlin Heidelberg for permission to include Helmut Thomä's 'Transference interpretations and reality', first published in Helmut Thomä and Horst Kächele, *Psychoanalytic Practice*, vol. 1, *Principles*, 1987, pp. 277–93.

ILLUSION AND
SPONTANEITY IN
PSYCHOANALYSIS

The essays in this book strike me as an invitation to reflect, as the contributors have done, on the analytic space. It is premised on an illusion maintained between patient and analyst. The transference has rapidly changing elements of fantasy and reality, of then and now. Within that space two selves explore and negotiate realities. One of those realities is the actual personality of the analyst and the actual conscious and unconscious responses which eventually get conveyed in one way or another.

The essays collected in John Klauber's *Difficulties in the Analytic Encounter* (New York: Jason Aronson, 1981) explore the analytic situation, technique and the analyst. Four of the ten chapters in the present book carry these themes further and express them more boldly. Klauber died while preparing them as part of a series for the Freud Memorial Visiting Professorship at University College London, and the first, his Inaugural Lecture, was delivered by Eric Rayner six weeks after he died.

This book owes its existence to the devotion of John

Klauber's widow, to the good offices of Neville Symington
and to Mark Paterson, Klauber's literary agent. Ruth
Brook Klauber was right to believe that the lectures her
husband had prepared should not languish for the cruel
and arbitrary reason that before he died he had written
too few to make a book of decent length.

When Neville Symington persuaded me to read the
lectures I agreed that they should be published but could
not see my way around the commercial problem of
making a proper book. The gentle persistence of Mark
Paterson kept me thinking about the problem. (He has
been helpful to Free Association Books in many ways,
including the obtaining of the rights to do a paperback
reprint of Klauber's *Difficulties* in association with
Maresfield Library, 1986.)

It eventually occurred to me that Klauber was reflecting
an important point of view – perhaps it should be called
a tonality – about the psychoanalytic relationship. It is
hard to describe; hence this hybrid – part Klauber's
lectures and part a collection of papers by admirers of his
whose approaches are resonant with his ideas.

One feature is that the analytic relationship derives its
significance from being a certain sort of human relationship. This is a truism but an important one in asserting
the place of psychoanalysis in a humanistic tradition in
contrast with various scientisms, whether structuralist,
ego-psychological or instinctual. Another and closely
related feature is civility as a surer guide than orthodoxy.
A third aspect is strait-jacketed in the fashionable concept
of 'countertransference' and refers to the complex inter-
relations in the analytic situation, the reflections on the
conscious and unconscious feelings which are becoming
increasingly important in the way psychoanalysis is conceived and practised. Many have attempted to describe
these matters in metapsychological terms. Part of what
is so refreshing about Klauber's writing is that he is
straightforward about the fact that the relationships are
personal ones, and the illumination of them benefits
from avoiding the defensive representation of them as

something impersonal. Many practitioners have come to
see countertransference, properly handled, as a positive
rather than a negative factor in the analytic relationship,
but only a few have begun to write about it in a way
which is commensurate with that point of view. Klauber
has led the way in this and writes clearly about matters
which are inherently unclear, e.g., 'the area of incompletely framed communication' that cannot be captured
in notes or a tape recording; 'implicit concepts with which
the analyst works'.

In his illuminating and thoughtful essay, Neville
Symington rounds out Klauber's philosophy of psychoanalysis and its influence on his own work. He links
and contrasts the present lectures with the themes of
Difficulties, seeing Klauber's concept of spontaneity as
analogous to Freud's 'free-floating attention' and Bion's
'reverie'.

In his essay on the freedom of the will, Roger Kennedy,
who was a training analysand of Klauber's, offers a gentle
exploration of the space within which spontaneity can
operate for the analyst and for the patient.

Nicole Berry writes about what happens at the end of
analysis, a time when increased spontaneity goes hand in
hand with the disciplined relinquishing of the transference
illusion, along with the realization of the benefits of
becoming a person who is *not* in analysis. Her rich and
touching case studies sparkle with insights, especially
about the analyst's mourning processes, and the uniquely
rich work that can be done in the last phase.

Patrick Casement gives us lovely examples of how
orthodoxy can lead to stasis or trauma. He emphasizes
the need for flexibility in, for example, self-revelation, the
management of silences, and responding (or not) to direct
requests by the patient. He also shows just how subtle
and delicate the role requirements in the transference can
be, as in the case of one patient who wanted him to survive
– but only *just*.

The last two papers, along with that of Nicole Berry,
are written by Continental admirers of John Klauber's

x work. Daniel Widlöcher carefully considers the metaphysical consequences in classical Freudian terms of lowering the barrier between the concept of ego and that of the self. He explores the tendencies that separate the theoretical and structural concept of ego from the lay concept of the self on which Klauber's humanistic philosophy of psychoanalysis depends.

Helmut Thomä returns to a common source of his and Klauber's development – reflections on the 'reality' of the psychoanalytic situation. He provides a sustained reflection on James Strachey's classical papers which began to challenge the orthodox view of the analyst as a smooth mirror. Every analyst works in a way that conforms to his personality, but the problem of reality – the personal influence and realistic perceptions of the analyst – has to be reinterpreted in the light of the nature of the transference illusion.

As Neville Symington points out, John Klauber declined to be a systematizer. He did so in the name of a space for spontaneous selves – people – to find their own way in analysis and beyond. As I experience them, all of the essays in this book have that same goal: they are enabling. I am reminded of F. R. Leavis's description of the essence of the literary critic's interpretations: 'This is so; isn't it?' And he listened for the reply.

Robert M. Young, Publisher

Lecture 1

THE ROLE OF ILLUSION IN THE PSYCHOANALYTIC CURE

John Klauber

C URE BY TRUTH and by illusion are closely inter-
woven at the heart of psychoanalysis: the technique of psychoanalysis depends crucially on a
phenomenon evoked by an act of psychic prestidigitation.
That the technique depended on such an act was not
consciously realized by Freud at first, though the adoption
of the hypnotist's setting of the couch – with the analyst
sitting out of the patient's view, accompanied at first by
pressing the patient's head to evoke memories – suggests
that he may have had some subliminal awareness of it.

After all, quasi-magical techniques were in the air:
hypnotism itself, and experiments in the occult. Pierre
Janet (quoted in Ellenberger, p. 367) had already introduced himself consciously into his patients' hallucinations
and acted a role there. The act of psychic prestidigitation
to which I am referring is the evocation, by the setting
of psychoanalysis, of the phenomenon of transference,
which Jung (1921) described, to Freud's satisfaction, as
the alpha and omega of psychoanalytic treatment. This is
the area in which truth and illusion mingle inextricably,

2   and the area where the constant attempt to extricate one from the other has increasingly become the main focus of therapy.

I ought to sketch out a brief description of transference. As used in psychoanalytic treatment, the transference refers to the displacement of conflictual wishes from an earlier relationship into the relationship with the analyst. Perhaps all our relationships have an important element of transference; but the analytic set-up of free association and the couch, designed to diminish the pull of reality, causes the transference elements to be experienced more sharply.

To give examples: a migrant from a less developed community who has guiltily settled in England cannot resist the fantasy that the analyst is a cart driver with a whip, and thinks he can smell garlic on his breath; a woman athlete, abandonded by her mother at eighteen months but warmly loved and encouraged by her grand-mother, finds her portly, middle-aged male analyst almost irresistible sexually; a man whose seductive actress-mother was always leaving him as a child is constantly afraid that the analyst will throw him out; a man with a phobia of eating in childhood, and a tendency to indulge himself in adult life, cannot rid himself of the strange compulsive thought, 'Do analysts eat?'

The earliest recognized and unexpected form of trans-ference was the falling in love of a woman patient with a male therapist – with Breuer, in fact, and then Freud (Breuer and Freud, 1893–5, pp. 21–47). (Freud does not report the analysis of a male patient until 1909 (Freud, 1909).) It became apparent that this guilty falling in love had its precursor in the patient's wishes in childhood in relation to her father, and her fears of punishment by her mother – that is, in the normal culmination of the sexual development of the earliest years in the Oedipus complex. But by the early 1900s this would already have appeared to be a simplistic statement of the complexities of relation-ship which go to make the transference.

Freud came to see that the transference uses a multi-

plicity of childhood relationships and often expresses
them indirectly via other relationships, that it 'uses reality
very skilfully', and that defences against the transference
wishes are as important as the wishes themselves. The
patient can thus be seen as repeating his past conflicts in
a new and intensely felt relationship with the analyst,
where they can be studied and resolved as their incon-
gruity becomes manifest. By 1912 Freud was stating that
the battles of analysis were fought out more and more
during its course on the field of transference (1912a,
p. 104). Today, all psychoanalysts take up the manifestations of transference from the start.

I will give one brief example to illustrate how transference reveals itself from the beginning and can be interpreted. A man who was successful in a quite different
profession decided he wanted to train as a psychoanalyst.
During the interview he remarked that his experiences in
a recent climbing expedition had convinced him that
people were often called brave when in fact they were
suicidal. What he was telling me about his life situation
was that in giving up his career for a climbing expedition
in psychoanalysis, he did not know whether he was being
brave or suicidal, and he was appealing to me quite
realistically as a psychoanalyst to help him determine
which it was. But behind this in the transference, as it
turned out, he was putting me in the position of his elder
brother, who had lured him on towards false ideals and
squashed him whenever he tried to express his true
personality. He was now watching me to see whether I
would lure him on to false ideals or allow him to express
his personality. Both could be represented by training to
be a psychoanalyst, and true and illusory ideals were
intertwined in a complex way in the aspiration.

Transference arises as a result of conflict, and in this
example you can clearly see the resistance to becoming a
psychoanalyst as well as the desire for it. Now transference is classically described as a resistance to analysis: it
is a resistance because it is a way of behaving instead of
remembering. But it immediately strikes one as a little

4   pejorative to call transference a resistance when the whole analytic set-up is designed to induce it. After all, the development of transference manifestations – and particularly, as the analysis proceeds, the development of the neurotic conflict itself in relation to the analyst (that exacerbated form of transference known as transference neurosis) – means that the patient is showing the analyst his illness in the only way he can, and experiencing it and watching it at the same time. The development of transference, distressing as some of the forms in which it shows itself may occasionally be, is an invitation to the analyst to help his patient discriminate the illusory from the real at an increasingly complex psychological depth, and is for this reason a therapeutic experience. It was also noted long ago by Freud that as the neurotic conflict concentrates itself in the transference neurosis the patient's difficulties in his outside life are reduced.

It might be truer to say that, therapeutic as the transference experience is, there is an element in both patient and analyst which resists it. Whatever varied motives the analyst's sitting behind the couch serves – and its main conscious *raison d'être* is to activate Freud's Magic Lantern (see Moss, 1963) for the manifestation of transference – it is also true that the analyst's calm, mirror-like attitude serves to protect him from the patient's emotions. (In earlier days some analysts even wore white coats.) I suspect that psychoanalytic theory sees the transference as primarily a resistance precisely because it is irresistible, and because both patient and analyst have such difficulty in relinquishing the relationship formed in the context of transference. Indeed the danger of being carried away by emotion is a constant threat to both analyst and patient in their intimate relationship, and the jokes that are made about analysis – not to mention occasional unfortunate occurrences – testify to it. The prototype of such jokes is the male analyst who refuses a request by a woman patient with the words, 'I shouldn't even be on the couch with you'.

Almost every patient enters analysis reluctantly, and

his reluctance is articulated on two limbs. One is his fear of surrendering to the attraction of pure feeling, the other is his fear of being deprived of feeling. Two characters in Shaw's *Major Barbara* present the problem well: Todger Fairmile, the music hall wrestler, of whom Barbara reports that he 'wrestled against the Jap till his arm was going to break, but he wrestled against his salvation till his heart was going to break'; and Barbara's father, Andrew Undershaft, who has known suffering as a foundling and an East Ender who understands the fear of losing feeling, and quietly says to her, 'You have learnt something, that always feels at first as though you had lost something' (1905, Act 3, p. 156).

Psychoanalysis began with the appreciation of the therapeutic effectiveness of discharging emotion – with the relief of hysterical symptoms by the cathartic method. Perhaps this has been in some respects undervalued since interpretation and understanding gained pride of place over the release of repressed memories. Of course for several decades the aim of interpretation was regarded as the facilitation of this release, an aspiration which failed to recognize the evident truth that it remained largely an unrealizable ideal. But authors such as Ernst Kris (1956a, b) have made us a little wary even of the ideal, making it clear that the sudden release of repressed memories has a traumatic quality. It results in the idealization of analysis, with the longing for another magic moment, and therefore may be regarded, at least in theory, as a sign of insufficiently subtle analysis of the defences holding the memories out of consciousness. If the defences are adequately analysed the memories are not experienced by the patient as repressed.

Freud had already recognized that this type of recall was a sign that the analysis was nearing completion. Modern analysis rests more on reconstruction and particularly reconstruction from the transference, with less insistence on direct confirmation by memory. In Bernfeld's words, 'It does not so much reconstruct events as build a model of the mind' (Bernfeld, 1932). The ideal

6   model of analysis had already in Freud's day undergone a shift of emphasis from the direct emotional results of recall, in favour of the growth of the synthetic functions of the personality.

Rather than the English psychological jargon, 'Where Id was there shall Ego be' (1933, p. 80), which is supposed to represent Freud's direct and simple German, I would prefer to translate 'Wo Es war soll Ich werden' as 'What was It must become Me'. But it would be just as true to say of our patients, all of whom suffer predominantly from inhibitions, that their ideal of therapy is the converse – that 'What was Me should become It'. This is what the transference experience gives them.

I am now approaching the crux of my lecture. It is the nature and value of the therapeutic madness called transference induced by psychoanalysis. People will immediately object that I exaggerate if I call it madness. I agree that I exaggerate. The transference is marked by a striking invasion of the patient's normal sense of reality, and it displays confusional, and even in normal subjects occasionally delusional features, but analysis would be impossible unless sanity were constantly regained. However, I do not wish to describe the forces that remain in control. I wish to describe the therapeutic value of the surrender to transference. Perhaps illusion would be a more suitable word than madness, especially if you will accept a tentative definition of illusion as a false belief accompanied by uncertainty as to whether it should be given credence. An illusion is produced by the break-through of unconscious emotion without consciousness surrendering to it completely. An illusion is a waking dream but somewhat less convincing.

There can be few cultures which have failed to recognize that dreams are valuable. In one way or another it has always been realized that they tell us something that we did not previously know about our feelings, and we hasten to communicate our dreams to those with whom we are intimate and get their reaction. The dream of the

transference illusion confuses an old relationship with
a new one, and therefore makes a comparison. The
transference illusion is not simply a false perception or a
false belief, but the manifestation of the similarity of the
subjective experience aroused by an event in the past and
in the present. The illusion therefore represents a new
piece of understanding, expressing itself not in the
language of logical thought, but in that of artistic
creativity.

We do not normally explain the patient's illusions as
comparisons. In the theory and practice of psychoanalysis
we are preoccupied with the patient's epidiascope, with
which he projects his stock of emotional slides onto the
analyst. We still try essentially to represent the analyst as
a blank screen, though this has been modified in the last
thirty years by the analysis of what is inexactly called the
analyst's countertransference, that is to say, his response.
I do not wish to question the general validity of this
approach which has become the backbone of psychoanalytic technique. And the strength of the patient's illness,
determined by the strength of his unresolved feelings,
determines the inevitability of this projection. The transference illusion reduces his peripheral thoughts and his
reactions to individual experiences to a common emotional bedrock.

Now when we know our feelings, we feel more real.
Of course, coming to know our feelings is a process of
discrimination. But it is the illusion in psychoanalysis that
first brings the patient in touch with the reality of his
feelings, and I think that this is a very important reason
why patients are so reluctant after analysis to acknowledge the illusory content of their transference. Dionysus
is a frightening god. They would much rather explain
how in reality their analyst was exactly as they perceived
him. And I think that in overstressing the value of
interpretation, as in my opinion many analysts do –
though Ferenczi, Michael Balint and Winnicott belonged
to a different stream – psychoanalysts betray the same

8   fear as their patients of the clarifying emotional power of illusion.

The illusion, then, makes the patient feel more real and puts more emotion at his disposal. It has done him a valuable service, because we need access to illusions and dreams to live. Freud pointed out, for instance, that falling in love shows many of the characteristics of mental abnormality. We cannot live by reality alone. We need the illusions which touch reality 'with a celestial light'. That is why religion is so important in all societies, not excluding – however much we may object to religion – the esoteric forms that often pervade scientific societies. Its illusions give us the emotional courage to live beyond reality. It directs our faith, which Tolstoy (1903) defined as 'the force whereby we live'. In psychoanalysis the transference not only helps the patient to discriminate, but to imagine.

With this little hymn to the irrational, I am introducing my next point about the value of the transference experience. The feelings that are mustered by the analytic set-up, and experienced in relation to the analyst, are frustrated by him, since what the analyst does is largely to interpret. Although he will also show his human feelings and understanding in a wider context than that of pure interpretation, his analytic skill, and, I suspect, his clinical success, can be measured by the degree to which his humanity is co-ordinated with his analytic function. Because the patient is forced by the analyst's interpretations to learn instead of to feel, he has to use the emotion aroused by analysis elsewhere.

I will quote what a woman in her thirties, speaking of a quite new phase of tenderness between herself and her lover of many years' standing, said to me, as I noted it down immediately after the session. 'I don't know whether I love him more because I love you. I don't know whether I substitute him for you. I think that because I trust you I can love him.' She then said, 'Love comes

through knowing oneself. It may refer to God or to
another person. But it is truth.'

What was truth and what was illusion in her attitude, and how were they related? Did she love me or did she only love a mother or a father from early childhood, as her memories of them came nearer to consciousness in the analysis and were projected on to me? Was the new tenderness in her relationship with her lover based on a transference of her feelings for an analyst whom she was idealizing and who was responding to her idealization? Or did a new absence of fear in her relationship with me (which was also a feature of that phase of the analysis) release tender feelings for me which she could no longer control, so that she could only solve the problem of her frustration by displacing them on to her lover?

If loving me enabled her to love him more, then it may well have been, as she suspected, that he received what was really meant for me. Indeed, in part, it must have been so, because she not infrequently confused us. But if she loved him more because she trusted me, then her trusting me enabled her to make a generalization to the effect that 'Men with certain characteristics can after all be trusted'. This would imply no confusion. This new trust would have removed her fear of him, and therefore her hostility, and thus allowed her for the first time to love him without ambivalence.

One of the problems of truth and illusion in transference love was broached by Freud in 1915 (1915a, p. 168) when he asked if this love was 'genuine', in a paper remarkable in its time for its capacity to deal coolly with a scandalous subject, but open to criticism today. He concluded that it was as genuine as any; if it had clear sources in the infantile, so does all falling in love. That transference love was often used as a resistance against being analysed was neither here nor there except for the technical difficulty of handling it. And he warned analysts that a woman patient would not take more kindly to her love being scorned than any other woman.

Freud did not discuss in any detail the difficulties that

10   might arise if patients fell 'genuinely' in love with their analysts. For him it was the unavoidable consequence of a medical situation and had to be accepted as such. This assumed, of course, in Freud's simile, that the analyst could be relied on not to behave like the joker in the dog race for a garland of sausages, who spoilt the race by throwing a single sausage on to the track. The woman would be free to use her newly won capacity for love in the service of her ordinary life.

That is perhaps the situation that my patient was describing. That is to say, the transference illusion is of value not only as a technical aid to the resolution of the conflict that gives rise to it, but because the illusion can be carried on into life to give a new impetus to relationships and ideals with a less direct relationship to the original conflict.

The primary therapeutic illusion that enables the patient to equate one love object with another is that time does not exist. It is a similar therapeutic illusion to that which enabled the narrator of A la recherche du temps perdu to know that he would become a great writer, when he rescued the essence of an experience 'from the order of time'. The narrator equates the sensation of the unevenness of the paving stones in the courtyard of the Princesse de Guermantes on his way to her matinée with the unevenness of the paving stones in St Mark's Baptistry in Venice; and the tinkle of the spoon against the plate, when he enters the Library, with the sound of the hammer against the wheels of the railway train stopped near a little wood. The patient, like Proust, has the illusion as the result of 'involuntary memory' that his experience exists outside time, and Freud, and psychoanalysts in general (not to mention some idealist philosophers of history), have become the victims and the beneficiaries of the same illusion.

The concept that experiences can be repeated is used in psychoanalysis as though Heraclitus had never lived. For instance, Freud defined happiness as the fulfilment of a childhood wish. But a childhood wish is never exactly

fulfilled – only the transformed derivative of a childhood
wish – and I believe that it brings joy and satisfaction,
rather than happiness. In fact, although Freud defines the
unconscious as being timeless – in spite of the many
unconscious biological clocks that we have in our body
– the recognition of the similarity of an emotional experience in time is immediately followed by an activation of
the secondary process which evaluates the experience and
sets new ideals. It is what Proust called 'the miracle of an
analogy' that liberates, and allows each memory, in the
words of Howard Moss (1963), to be 'transfigured by the
velocity of the future'.

I think that this is central to the concept of psychoanalytic cure. The experience of timelessness is a mystical
experience of profound value, and an essential prerequi-
site of cure, but it is not the cure itself. Nor does the cure
consist only in the secondary evaluation of the primary
emotional experience. The cure consists in the fact that the
patient's comparison and differentiation of the experience
makes possible a new development, in which he can again
lose the power of discrimination in terms of a new unconscious synthesis of reality and illusion.

It is the continuity of this process which is at the centre
of the patient's development, and it begins more than it
ends with the analysis. During the time patient and analyst
are together, a way of looking at the analytic experiences
is unconsciously agreed between them. This area of
common understanding which enables the analysis to
proceed is, by the fact that two separate personalities are
involved, of necessity limited. In my view, the patient can
only develop his own analysis fully when he is free from
the analyst, and from what has been called 'the modelling
myth' in an unpublished contribution by Waldemar
Zusman (n.d.).

It is therefore precisely his secondary criticism of his
original analytic experiences and their interpretation
which enables his real development as an individual, and
not as a disciple, to take place. This is, of course, easier
for the ordinary run of patients to accomplish than it is

12 for those patients who are also psychoanalytic trainees, and will have to continue to associate with their former analysts.

I think that it was of this development that my patient spoke, when she said that knowing oneself could be equated with love; and that this love did not possess an inherent direction, but might be for God, or for another person. I think that when she spoke of God she referred to a *logos*, an ordering principle which comes from self-scrutiny, leading to self-knowledge. I think she spoke of something like Proust's 'miracle of an analogy', and meant that as one discriminates one's feelings better, they can also be experienced more sharply and therefore allow one to love another person or an ideal wholeheartedly. I think she spoke of the inner world and its possibilities that only self-knowledge, free from dependency on other mortals, can create. She was speaking of her own inner order, and I have been attempting to translate what she described into a theory of psychoanalytic therapy. In psychoanalysis the *logos*, the Word, is inevitably made Flesh by the transference. This is another therapeutic illusion; but in a successful analysis the Flesh again becomes the Word.

Lecture 2

TRUTH AND ILLUSION IN THE PATIENT'S SYMPTOMS

John Klauber

IN THE FIRST LECTURE I discussed the interrelationship of truth and illusion in the patient's attitude to the analyst – how feelings from childhood, originally for other love objects, attach themselves to the present relationship, become intertwined with it, and are modified by it. In this lecture I wish to discuss the relationship of truth and illusion in the picture that a person forms of himself, as it is revealed in the symptoms that cause him to seek relief.

I will again start with two examples. An attractive woman in her mid-thirties, with two teenage children, came to consultation for a flying phobia. Her husband was an extremely successful business man – he was just breaking the millionaire barrier. Recently he had wished her to fly home with him from abroad, but she had found herself unable to do so. Instead she had had to come the long way back by sea. This symptom by itself would scarcely seem an indication for such a lengthy procedure as psychoanalysis, but the situation was clearly more complicated. Her husband had for some time been having psychotherapeutic help from the very experienced psychiatrist who referred her. The psychiatrist had kept his patient's confidence concerning his reasons for seeking treatment, but he did feel able to give me what information he had about the wife. She was suffering, he thought, from guilt 'over some little affair'. The analysis that presented with a minor symptom was to prove an exceedingly long one with only a partial therapeutic result, even though the presenting symptom of the flying phobia cleared up without much difficulty.

What did the phobia mean? In what way did it represent truth about herself, and in what way illusion? It represented the truth that she could no longer fly home with her husband at a number of symbolic levels of meaning. There was soon to be no home; her husband was already having an affair with another woman for whom he eventually left her, but his wife tried hard to deny this reality. Her symptom recognized its truth while her consciousness did not. Her husband's psychiatrist told me afterwards that the husband had been 'split right down the middle' by his conflict. The enormous sexual excitement that she had experienced with him when she 'took off' was misplaced in the sense that her husband, as she eventually learnt, participated in it so little internally that his marriage to her may even have made him physically ill, or apparently physically ill – in spite of its seeming to her, and to the outside world, to be a good one. When the final separation came my patient, at decent intervals, started a number of promising affairs, and even became engaged to be married, but every attempt at a relationship crashed. She could not make a home with any man because after a time she always developed a conviction that he was two-timing her with another woman, and made his life such a misery that he left her – I think with relief that he had escaped being trapped into a marriage with someone who, despite her abundant supply of common sense, gradually revealed herself to be insane in one area.

The flying phobia certainly had roots in the sort of

childhood experiences which would be expected in Freudian theory: experiences of dancing, of swinging once
resulting in an accident, of feeling too short for sexual
relations with her father – in short, of sexual excitement
in early childhood and the fear of it. It crystallized when
she was faced with a moment of truth of her adult life,
that is, when she was about to experience disappointment
from the man she loved and to whom she had devoted
her youth. The truth was that she was to prove incapable
of ever flying again in any love relationship. The illusion
in the symptom lay in her belief that it was flying in an
aeroplane that she was afraid of; and in her denial that
she was in a serious crisis with her husband, whose ascent
to riches and taste for a new way of life disinclined his
wife, whose tastes were more modest, to fly with him
socially or physically.

In this instance the symptom was an illusion – not even
a long-standing illusion – which masked the reality of her
situation. The relationship of symptom to psychological
reality may sometimes be more direct. A man presented
with a feeling which dominated him even though he could
not exactly define it; his nearest approach was to say that
it was similar to William Cowper's idea (quoted in Cecil,
pp. 67–8) that he was damned. At the same time he felt
himself to be more and more taken over by his father's
character – a man whom he described as 'an ageless being
from another world', in fact from the world that had
existed before 1914. His ability to have sexual relations
with his wife had also deserted him; instead he could only
be interested in women 'in severely masculine clothes'.
This man did not feel damned in any religious sense of
the word, and he was not consciously religious. But his
symptom made a fairly clear comment on the life he was
leading and where it was leading him. At different times
he expressed his fears of doom in direct and realistic
terms; at other times his symptom overwhelmed him. He
was possessed by a plan to revive an industrial process
from another age, and to do so against the whole development of modern industry and commerce. This was not a

16 mad idea, and in fact he had considerable success with it. But he felt that this was only one of the ways in which he was becoming increasingly isolated from the modern world – in his literary and personal tastes, such as his dislike of modern transport. He was increasingly taken over by the legends propagated in his childhood by his 'ageless' father and which he no longer wished to resist. However, he was disturbed by his increasing inability to turn to women, whom he began to despise. That is to say, his symptom represented a partial escape from his predicament and not a total denial of it. To the outward eye, he was on the verge of a depressive psychosis with delusions, whereas the woman was outwardly only neurotic. The analysis of the acutely ill man, however, proved more successful than that of the woman with her available common sense.

But was it successful because his appreciation of his condition was more direct? Certainly the availability of emotions is an important criterion for psychoanalysis, the aim of which is to regain past time and render its lost emotions accessible to the ego. But emotions, when strong enough, are also what drive people insane. It is, for instance, such an emotion as unbearable pain and grief over responsibility for the destruction of his love objects which makes a man develop a symptom like the delusion that he is damned. It is the torment of jealousy over the loss of a man without whom she feels she cannot live that makes a woman develop the delusion that everyone with whom she has a relationship is betraying her. And it is the strength of unresolved emotion from childhood which predisposes a person to such a loss of control in adult life. The success of analysis may therefore in principle be predicted by the balance between the accessibility of emotion and the ability of the ego to handle it. I say 'in principle' because the actual balance between emotion and the capacity to handle it is not always easy to determine. One can embark on an analysis with a patient, like the woman with the flying phobia – who appears to be only mildly ill, and quite approachable, and who does not seem to be flooded by her emotions – and hesitate unnecessarily with a patient who seems to be on the verge of a depressive breakdown.

With the hindsight which our patients usually expect will be available to us as foresight one can usually see where one went wrong. The decisive factor is concerned with the patient's will or, in psychological jargon, his motivation. This is, in part, related to his degree of suffering but is not identical with it. It is the degree of his inner determination and confidence that he can master his conflict or despair and win a new stability. This, far more than for economic reasons (though they are important), is why our patients are mostly rather successful people who have made something of their lives.

What I am saying is that a person's suitability for psychoanalysis depends upon the availability of his emotions, but it is his inability to bear these emotions that gives him his symptoms. The capacity to benefit from analysis is therefore basically the capacity to replace illusion with painful truth. That is why Freud said early in his career (Breuer and Freud, 1893–5, p. 305) that all we can do is transform 'hysterical misery into common unhappiness'. However, I do not think that is quite true.

The path to facing emotions successfully is more complex, more devious than it might seem from my description. If it were taken unmodified it would imply that the patient's will, operating with the analyst's help, would cause the repressed emotions to express themselves even more directly in the transference and that the analysis of the transference would be the analysis of the neurosis. Indeed that is basic theory. The artificial neurosis induced by the technique of analysis would correspond with the true neurotic conflict underlying the disturbance in the patient's life. But, as in economics, basic theory is only a general guide to what happens, even though it accounts for a lot. The man who was damned could not be immediately saved by analysis; he had to be damned in analysis too. He had friends who had benefited from analysis, he said, but of course it went wrong for him – or so he maintained for a long time. Other people might enjoy it, but for him it was a torment. Similarly, the woman who could not fly with her husband could not fly with her analyst, or rather flew off at a tangent from any direction he took; with the result that she complained constantly both that she could never talk about the things she wanted to talk about, and that the analyst tried to direct her thoughts.

Both patients were transferring feelings from childhood. The damned patient had found it impossible as a child to make any reciprocal relationship. At home he had been a slave; and at school he won adherents rather than friends, so that he gradually withdrew into a world of his own in which he was a potentate administering imaginary empires. The woman had been utterly confused by what felt like betrayal by her main parental love objects, and did not know where her loyalties lay.

You may have noticed that in both these instances I have illustrated the transference from events which do not belong exclusively to the earliest period of childhood. They come from a period of the child's life when its character was already formed or forming. That is to say, what was being transferred was not a simple reaction to experience. It was a reaction to experience already mixed with the solutions which the child was finding most suited to its individual needs, whether these are withdrawal into an imaginary life as a potentate, or the simpler emotional defence of confusion.

Indeed it is impossible for an actual experience of the past to be transferred or 'relived' in the present, as the phrase has it. That has been known, if one thinks about it, since Heraclitus, and no doubt before. One cannot react to the analyst's interpretations as if they were breast milk because they are not breast milk, and they affect one's adult ears and mind, not one's baby mind and stomach. One can only react to them as if one were so

engrossed in memories of breastfeeding and in fantasies about it that one could not wait to get them going. When the woman with the flying phobia 're-experienced' her memory of falling off a swing she stumbled on the stairs. There was not a great deal of choice as to how she might re-enact it in relation to the session. But it was not a reliving. It was a re-edition, a readaptation of the experience to present conditions at an appropriate moment before the session in which she would then struggle with its meaning for her.

That is to say, the transference neurosis is not a direct repetition of events, or even experiences, but a constructive fiction devised by the patient. But not only devised by the patient. The transference neurosis must be one that the analyst can use skilfully. Some forms of behaviour will be more acceptable to one analyst than to another. However well developed the analyst's powers of self-analysis may be, he remains an individual with his individual talents and disabilities, spontaneous likes and dislikes, his personality favouring more reflection or the expression of emotion; more at ease with minor delinquency, say, or put off by it; more or less naturally sympathetic to perverse sexuality; more or less able to stand attacks on a beloved intellectual leader – Freud or Melanie Klein or Jacques Lacan perhaps – or wanting to put the patient right as well as to analyse him.

For all these reasons the transference is produced, as Waldemar Zusman pointed out in some interesting comments at the International Psychoanalytic Congress in 1979* by the combined interplay of the analyst's and the patient's needs. This is supported by the well-known fact that different attitudes are as often transferred as similar ones when a patient begins a new analysis with a fresh analyst; and it means that the theory that it is the gradual expression of emotional truth in the transference, and its integration into the ego, that results in cure has to be examined in the light of our methods of eliciting that

* [Dr Zusman was the respondent to papers on 'The value of reconstruction in the psychoanalysis of adults'. His remarks are unpublished – Ed.]

20   truth. What is the truth that is being expressed, and what is the truth that is being left out? Could it be that it is an illusion that the analysis of the transference – and more particularly the exacerbation of the conflicts inherent in it as they express themselves in relation to the treatment – is the alpha and omega of psychoanalysis?

This question was not directly raised by Freud, but he clearly stated in 1912 that the battle of transference analysis was not necessarily fought out on the ground that was developmentally most crucial (1912a, p. 104). Doubt that the analysis of the transference was always, or even usually, the omega of an analysis, even if it was the alpha, is clearly implied in the last clinical paper Freud wrote, 'Analysis terminable and interminable', published in 1937. In it he speaks of a successful analyst, now known to have been the great Hungarian analyst Sandor Ferenczi, who reproached him for not having detected and analysed his hostile feelings or, as they are technically called in this area, his negative transference (1937a, p. 221). Freud defended himself on the grounds that at the time of the analysis there were no signs of it, at least with 'the limited horizon of analysis in those early days', and in any case, even if there had been, it would have been impossible to activate the negative transference except by some unfriendly act.

This is a long way from psychoanalysis today, which automatically looks for the patient's ambivalence and brings his negative feelings to consciousness by the interpretation of signs which previously went unnoticed. The story and the subsequent development of technique confirm that the transference neurosis is not simply an inevitable phenomenon bearing inevitable character- istics; it is also what a particular analyst can see and handle and what the patient can bring to him. Ferenczi was right. Freud should have seen his negative transfer- ence, and should have activated it by interpretation without the necessity of any unfriendly act. And who knows what analysts today ought to be doing that they have not yet learnt! It is a reassuring fact that many of us are smugly aware of the deficiencies in our own training analysts' technique, and reasonably secure in the hope that our own pupils will look back similarly on our own deficiencies.

The conclusion that I come to is that all psychoanalysis is inevitably incomplete. It is true that the analysis of the transference is the alpha and omega of psychoanalytic technique in the sense that it is the prime distinguishing feature of psychoanalysis: its most vivid means of reconstructing past experience; often its most convincing channel for interpretation; and always the essential guideline if disaster is to be avoided. However, it is an illusion that the transference represents a repetition of past experience; the transference is rather the patient's personal interpretation, and personal myth, of his past experience. It is therefore a myth that we can reliably reconstruct external events through the analysis of the transference, as Freud thought he did in the Wolf Man case (1918), or Marie Bonaparte was able to do for herself and confirm from her childhood diaries (1939). We may or may not succeed in this, but essentially we do something else. As Bernfeld saw in 1932, we do not so much reconstruct events as build a model of the mind.

It follows that it is a myth – to which I do not think many analysts would subscribe today – that analysis can ever be a complete cure. But it is true that the analysis of the transference gives a deeper insight, even if one more difficult to attain, than can be obtained by any other means.

3 Lecture 3
THE ROLE OF SPONTANEITY
IN PSYCHOANALYTIC THERAPY

John Klauber

PSYCHOANALYSIS was defined by Freud in the *Encyclopaedia Britannica* of 1926 in two ways: firstly as 'a particular method of treating nervous disorders', and secondly as 'the science of unconscious mental processes, which has also been appropriately described as "depth psychology" ' (1926a, p. 264). The first part of this definition implies a close relation to the art of medicine; the second a relationship closer to the science of psychology than to what has traditionally been regarded as the province of the science of medicine – although no successful practising doctor can fail to be something of an intuitive psychologist. But perhaps this definition of psychoanalysis, which Freud made exactly thirty years after he had coined the term, confirmed a certain tension between its practical and theoretical field of activity.

Freud introduces the definition by saying that in the course of time the word has come to have these two meanings; this lecture is about the relationship between the scientific theory which underlies psychoanalytic technique, and the practical actions of the psychoanalytic therapist who induces effective psychological changes in the patient. I am not going to attempt a scholarly exposition of how these divergencies developed, or examine in detail the dichotomy between theory and practice, which, in any case, I do not wish to exaggerate. All psychoanalytic therapy is broadly grounded in the psychoanalytic theory of psychology, even if its practitioners tend to apply the theory more intuitively than consciously. What I want to discuss instead is the comparative neglect of our intuitive ways of functioning in the theory of psychoanalysis, and, more controversially, the dangers of being too theoretically pure or theoretically impure.

Although the term was not coined until later, the psychoanalytic method was established with Breuer and Freud's 'Preliminary communication', 'On the psychical mechanism of hysterical phenomena', in 1893, expanded into their *Studies on Hysteria* of 1895 (Breuer and Freud, 1893–5). Commenting on this in his 'Autobiographical study' of 1925, Freud remarked that the theory 'hardly went beyond the direct description of the observations' (1925, p. 21). This may be regarded as broadly true of the beautiful descriptions in the case histories, with their culmination in the relief of symptoms following the release of repressed memories. But at the age of sixty-eight Freud seems to have lost the memory of the tremendous intellectual struggles – and of his discussions and arguments with Breuer – which were necessary to achieve even a comparatively simple clinical formulation; a formulation already significantly different, at least in Freud's view and in that of the early psychoanalysts, from the views of Janet or Moritz Benedikt.

The clinical concept which separated Breuer and Freud from Janet, and was later to separate Freud from Breuer, was of course the concept of defence. That is to say, the idea that the patient took an active if unconscious part in driving his memories out of consciousness, rather than that the memories dropped out of consciousness as a result of his psychasthenia. The theoretical propositions of the *Studies*, with their ideas of mental energy and the tendency of the organism to reduce the effects of any stimulus to a level of constancy, go far beyond what is necessarily implied by the clinical descriptions themselves. So a tendency to theorize beyond the immediate necessities of accounting for the clinical phenomena was established even before the name psychoanalysis was conceived.

But I am leading up to a different point. The clinical theory of psychoanalysis is essentially a historical theory. It relates the present symptoms to the past, while the recovery, if not exactly of the memories, then of the memories in their emotional context causes a re-evaluation and discharge of the emotions in the present. I will call this historical approach the vertical analysis, and will be contrasting it with what I will call the horizontal analysis, the latter being based on the transactions in the present which take place between patient and analyst.

The Freudian structure of the mind may be regarded as almost entirely vertical: the mind is constructed in layers from the surface to the depths, as Freud's definition of psychoanalysis indicates. The depths are the mental representatives of instincts, themselves conservative, as all inherited dispositions must be, and repetitive in their aims. These mental representatives are unconscious, impulsive, and primitive in the sense of showing mental characteristics which are archaic. They take no account of logic, time or reality. They represent the earlier stages of human development. For Freud children are primitive, and the primitive is a child.

The contrast is with the adult ability to assess reality, accommodate to it and control it. Between the two is a layer, still unconscious, which mediates the emerging instinctual impulses – arising either spontaneously through biological processes or evoked by stimuli that play on them – by making connections with current, realistic possibilities that allow the impulses to be expressed as acceptable conscious wishes. This is the preconscious, the mental area in which impulses are transformed by connecting links in thought which render them capable of becoming conscious and expressed in adaptive behaviour. There is a constant struggle between the upper and lower systems – a pressure for discharge from the lower impulsive system, and a pressure to keep out the primitive from the adult system.

Winnicott once said that the first psychoanalyst was the person who invented names. A name changes diffuse sensations into a psychic concept, meaning that it differentiates them or analyses. We know that the first person who gave names to things was God in the Garden of Eden and that his first patients got into serious trouble. So it was with Freud. He first thought that you could make a breach in the defensive system by naming what was in the lower system – which is often true, and perhaps made him feel like God.

But it was only partially true even in the first phase of psychoanalysis, when the recovery of repressed memories was the aim of therapy. We know from the Fliess letters how many patients he lost; the fact that Freud was naming the *modus operandi* of sexuality was no doubt an important contributory factor. (God had wisely refrained and it was the Serpent who sabotaged his plans.) It became increasingly recognized that memories were repressed, not simply because they were painful, but because they represented wishes based on unacceptable primitive sexual drives.

It was in 1905 that Freud formulated his famous dictum that neurosis is the negative of perversion (1905, p. 238). This realization altered the concept of therapy, which became grounded more on the recognition of the course of normal human development with its conflicts, and less on the more accidental current happenings which reactivated those conflicts. From being a therapy based primarily on the concept of psychic trauma, and the need to discharge strangulated affect, it became a therapy based on rendering the primitive constitutional drives acceptable to the ego. It gradually became more and more clear that if analysis was to be accepted by the patient, its technique must lay less emphasis on naming the contents of the unconscious system, and more on the analysis of the barriers against admitting these contents to consciousness.

Two developments were paramount in bringing about this change; both of them clearly demonstrated the validity of the vertical approach, but both also introduced much greater opportunities for horizontal or transactional interpretation. The first was the increasing importance attached to the interpretation of dreams. The patient's associations to dreams clearly led to the memory of the events and desires of early childhood, but also to the strength with which these tendencies had survived in the frustrations of the day preceding the dream. These could be interpreted not simply as survivals from a remote past, but as the active residues of the past in present relationships. Perhaps dream interpretation is acceptable because it makes not only children of us all but artists, prophets and philosophers as well.

Closely allied with this development was the interpretation of transference, that is, of the re-enactment towards the analyst of impulses, desires, thoughts and fantasies very similar to those which existed towards the important persons of childhood, and which had been rediscovered in dreams. With the increasingly sophisticated technique of transference and dream analysis, and the linking of the two, the vertical approach became intertwined with the horizontal. What had been experienced in the past was also being enacted in a relationship between two persons in the present. When a patient complained that the analyst talked too much, for instance, was the analyst really interrupting the patient all the time? Or was the patient unduly sensitive because he always wanted to shout other people down, perhaps just as his father had done, and would therefore let no one else get a word in? In sorting the problem out, the analyst had to take account of both the vertical and the horizontal dimension.

These developments in technique turned the attention of both patient and analyst from symptoms to character structure. The example that I have given, for instance, is clearly concerned with the problem of whether the patient habitually projects his aggressive impulses on to the outside world, in this case represented by the analyst. It raises the question of the psychology of the sensitive character and its relationship, first pointed out by Kraepelin, to paranoia. Such phenomena completely alter the role of the analyst. Instead of the analyst's interpretations being given in the form of explanations, they have to be given as attempts to understand a puzzling interaction. This means that the analyst has to be much less active than Freud was at the beginning in order to allow the patient's fantasies about him to develop fully. It is in essence a much gentler process, much more psychological, and much more time-consuming, and I think that the change in Freud's character from authoritarianism to understanding and humour is clearly shown in his sequence of case histories.

Although I have described the interaction with the world which comes into the province of psychoanalysis with dream interpretation and with the current interaction with the analyst (which has to be examined in transference analysis), I have said nothing which disturbs the basically vertical structure of Freudian psychology. It is, however, a very intrapsychic way of looking at the situation between patient and analyst. Ultimately it reduces analysis to the idea that the patient repeats his past and that the analyst's personality has little to do with the process. Indeed Alice and Michael Balint stated in 1939 that the development of the patient's transference proceeded almost independently of the analyst's personality.

There is a lot of truth in this, as every psychoanalyst who has had patients previously treated by someone else knows. Things look different for a time, but the same basic patterns usually repeat themselves. None the less, it is an unconvincing idea, not to mention dehumanizing, that nothing truly horizontal happens in the analysis. And here I want to bring in two considerations. The first is an intellectual critique of a concept which has become fundamental in psychoanalysis; the second is an anecdote from my own experience from which I have gradually drawn conclusions which I regard as important.

There was after the war what I would call a significant revolt against the purely intrapsychic view of the psychoanalytic process, though, as far as I know, it was never articulated as such. This was the development of a new view of countertransference, the concept that I will first explain and then criticize. It had always been recognized that the analyst must have human feelings about his patient, such as like or dislike, which could interfere with his objectivity. Since this emotional interference with his objectivity was regarded as rooted in his own past, it was recognized that the analyst also made a transference to the patients, and this was regarded as a pathological phenomenon which the analyst must neutralize by self-analysis. After the war it was primarily British psychoanalysts who began to recognize that the so-called countertransference could have a positive value. First Winnicott in 1947 courageously described his relationship with a patient whom he could not stand, and the therapeutic improvement which took place when, as a result of analytic work, it became possible for him to discuss the reasons for his reactions (Winnicott, 1949).

In 1950 Paula Heimann described the vague feelings of unease that she had about a patient's prospective marriage and the way in which these feelings, so far from being a transference on to the patient of (say) jealousy, gave her valuable objective cues to the psychological processes operating in the patient (Heimann, 1950). The value of countertransference became the great new psychoanalytic discovery, originally of the so-called Independent or Middle group of British psychoanalysts, gradually permeating the more traditional school of analysis, and being taken up not so much by Melanie Klein, but ever more enthusiastically by the Kleinian what does the patient do to the analyst or, in the jargon, project into him?

I would like to point out that the concepts of transference and countertransference are by no means on the same footing. They are not the reciprocals that the terms suggest. Transference comes largely from the past and is basically unjustified, even though, as I said in my first lecture (p. 3) quoting Freud, it 'uses reality very skilfully'. But nobody maintains that the patient's transference is an accurate indicator of what is going on in the analyst. Sometimes patients are perceptive and sometimes they are almost deluded, but, without discounting in any way their capacity for a good deal of objectivity in their assessment of their analyst, the transference has more to do with illusions from the past than with current reality. But you will already have noticed that the sense in which countertransference was elaborated as a concept after the war was exactly contrary. It used an old term, which had described a valid concept, and gave it a new meaning. The term remained the same, but its substance did not. Countertransference in this new sense is not transference, but unconscious assessment.

The anecdote that I want to tell may not seem at first to have much relevance. In 1961 the British Psycho-Analytical Society was requested to give a series of clinical seminars for the benefit of visiting psychoanalysts who would later proceed to the International Congress in Edinburgh. I was asked to give one of the seminars. I had no idea what to talk about as it had taken me eight years of full-time practice to learn to apply the vertical theory to the structure of a psychoanalytic session, and I had never given a paper in public. None the less, some intuition told me that this already had some element of originality, although by all reasonable standards it ought to have been plain sailing to any student by the time he qualified.

To my amazement the seminar was a great success and resulted in invitations to speak and publish abroad. Its theme seemed so elementary to me that I only dared to

30   publish my introductory talk in English* in a volume
     of selected papers twenty years later (Klauber, 1981,
     pp. 77–90). But the lesson is obvious even though it took
     a long time to dawn on me. If the application of basic
     Freudian metapsychology to a session struck an inter-
     national audience of psychoanalysts as new, then it was
     clear that there was a very curious dichotomy between
     theory and practice. Perhaps psychoanalysts operated
     the theory unconsciously – but then why did not its
     articulation strike them as banal? Perhaps it did not strike
     them as banal for the same reason that a centipede would
     not find it banal if the theory of walking were explained
     to him. But I don't think that this is the reason. The
     component parts of the vertical theory of psychoanalysis,
     and even their integration, are much less complicated
     than the theory of centipedal ambulation.

     I would suggest that the reason for the seminar's
     popularity was that it helped to resolve a number of
     confusions in the analyst's mind. Although the vertical
     theory is comparatively uncomplicated, there is always a
     problem of which part of it to apply. Should the analyst
     go first for the patient's anxiety? Or the continuity with
     the session before? Or the patient's emotional state? Or
     even for the relationship with the analyst himself? My
     paper ['The structure of the session as a guide to interpret-
     ation'] tried to give a structure of a logical kind to the
     session which took into account the development of
     Freud's thought during his lifetime and ended there. It
     suggested a scheme which started with his second anxiety
     theory of 1925 (Freud, 1926b), and said in effect: 'See
     what is making the patient anxious in his current situ-
     ation. See how this is reflected in his attitude to the
     analyst. See how he tries to avoid the anxiety. And then
     decide what the basic unconscious impulse is that is
     disturbing him.' It went from the surface to the depth in
     the later-Freudian way, and it emphasized the role of the
     transference as a current indicator of archaic conflicts.

* [First published in German. See Klauber, 1981, p. xi – Ed.]

But why did analysts need such a guide? I think it can only have been because all analysts do a great many things that are not in the book, and the seminar gave them the reassurance that it might not be too difficult – actually it is – to stick to the book. The seminar could at least be a guide for what they should be trying to do even if they were not entirely succeeding.

Here we come again to the horizontal analysis, for it is in fact impossible to work like a computer. Of course the analyst must do a great deal of thinking, but he must also act spontaneously if the analysis is to have any life. And when he reacts spontaneously, it may be the end product of the kind of thinking I described, or it may not. It is sometimes said that even if the analyst acts spontaneously, he should always be able to give a reason afterwards for what he has done. I don't believe that. I think it devalues the power of intuition too much. But I do think it is true that if he is too often unable to give a reason his analysis becomes wild, and that this is a danger that all analysts fear. The reason why we all take such long holidays, or do other work besides pure psychoanalysis is basically, in my opinion, because psychoanalysis demands more constant self-control than human nature is easily capable of.

The more spontaneous elements of the psychoanalytic procedure have received somewhat more detailed study in the last thirty-five years. There had always been a vague idea, started by Ferenczi, that the analyst's love cured the patient. I agree that psychoanalytic work is easier if one likes the patient. I am far from being one of those psychoanalysts who sometimes give the impression of believing that to like the patient is already an indicator of pathological countertransference; nor am I of the opinion of the analyst who announced that many of his patients complained that he had no sense of humour. Actually, he said, he had a very good sense of humour; it was just that he did not laugh in analysis. But I think we sentimentalize if we imagine that we love our patients; or at least, if we find we are starting to do so, it is time to watch out.

Franz Alexander to some extent revivified this notion with his idea of the 'corrective emotional experience' (1957); this is, however, already more sober. The non-moralizing attitude of the analyst is of great therapeutic value for the patient, and remains so even if most analysts are human enough to have occasional lapses. Sacha Nacht was also stressing a valid point in the 1960s when he stressed the importance for the patient of the presence of an analyst who tries to understand, even if analyst and patient are silent (Nacht, 1962, 1963, 1965). But his papers always aroused in me the uncomfortable feeling that he teetered on the edge of sentimentality. And when, a decade later, Ralph Greenson (1974) regarded the ability to love one's patients as part of a psychoanalyst's equipment for his job, I felt slightly alarmed.

Greenson's opinion was alarming because he had been a leader in an important attempt to isolate the non-transference elements of the analytic partnership responsible for the analytic work, from the irrational and emotional aspects represented by the transference. Such authors as Greenson and Elizabeth Zetzel in America, Heinrich Racker in Argentina and Denise Braunschweig in France had been responsible for the concept of the working or therapeutic alliance, and for defining the area of the operation of reality in the psychoanalytic relationship even if one or both partners were disturbed. This no doubt represented the gradual importation, into the sphere of technique, of the separation of the autonomous functions of the personality, on the part of the Viennese-American analysts of the forties and fifties, from 'the seething cauldron' of emotion.

In this country, in 1962, Bion described the operation of organized and unorganized types of thinking in the analyst's approach to the session and named them the beta and alpha elements (Bion, 1962). This was undoubtedly part of the horizontal analysis, representing the immediate impact of the patient on the analyst's current mentation before any historical assessment of his communication could be attempted. It recognized the importance of spontaneity, and I would like to end my lecture with an assessment of its role in keeping every analysis alive. It is spontaneity which allows the unconscious to work or, rather, which allows its most direct expression.

Freud thought that we are all endowed with an unconscious mechanism for understanding the unconscious of others. Be this as it may, the secondary mental processes certainly often inhibit our unconscious understanding as well as enhancing it. I know of no metapsychological proposition which demands that our spontaneous reactions should always be filtered through the secondary processes. In fact the spontaneous processes are responsible for the artistic and most creative aspects of the analysis, and can be almost as clever and perceptive in their operations as they are in dreams.

We need logic to think out our general understanding of what the patient is saying. But my model of 'The structure of the session as a guide to interpretation' in 1961 was incomplete because it is almost impossible to act on the logical analysis that one has made. At the last moment something intervenes and one finds oneself saying something at least a bit different, and occasionally quite different. This is how R. G. Collingwood (1938) defined the difference between art and craft. In most crafts the craftsman knows exactly the form his work will take before he commences it; Collingwood thought that it was the characteristic of art that the form changed as the artist executed his work.

Spontaneous thoughts occur to the analyst at all stages of his work. But it is the spontaneous communication of a new idea which evokes a spontaneous reaction in the patient and gives to both a feeling of a constructive session which will lead to further development. I have never recorded a session on tape, but I have often written it down as nearly as I could verbatim immediately after the session, and I have heard several tape recordings of group discussions. The logical content, of which one was

34   convinced at the time, is often strangely absent in the recording or in the notes which one is able to make afterwards.

We are dealing here with the partly formed thoughts which still reach for completion; what we think we understand is, as in Picasso's definition of art, the fiction by which we get nearer reality. I believe that the area of incompletely formed communication is an enormously creative one in psychoanalysis, and an area which we still need to study. It will not devalue the importance of the role of logical thinking, but I believe it will add immensely to our understanding of what happens in those analyses that go well and those that proceed only with difficulty.

Lecture 4

4

IMPLIED AND DENIED CONCEPTS IN THE THEORY OF PSYCHOANALYTIC THERAPY

John Klauber

A T THE END of my last lecture I was describing how the historical or vertical theory of psychoanalysis is modified in practice by the horizontal interaction between patient and analyst. I suggested that the study of what the analyst actually does might have important methodological implications. What I am now suggesting is that such a study might reveal the implicit concepts with which the analyst operates, the significance of which he minimizes, or of which he is unaware.

These implicit concepts may constitute a part of the particular mental set of an individual analyst, or they may characterize psychoanalysis as a whole. I think that the effort to make psychoanalysis into a science has tended to play down the importance of the individual personality of the analyst, in spite of the fact that the analyst's personality is clearly central to the technique. Several authors, including myself, have pointed this out, but it seems to need constant reiteration. Freud recommended that the analyst should listen to his patient with evenly free-floating attention, the analyst's counterpart to the patient's free associations (1912b, p. 111). Now every patient's free associations follow a very definite character pattern, and almost any session has a form and content specific for that patient. I remember Cecily de Monchaux – who worked for many years in the Psychology Department of University College – pointing out, in an unpublished paper given to the British Psycho-Analytical Society about one patient, that the pattern of the session repeated the patient's life history.

It cannot be true that the analyst's response to each of his patients is as stereotyped as that of the patient, who is only concerned with one analysis and one analyst. None the less it is true, as Michael Balint (1968) pointed out, that each analyst has his atmosphere which is easily recognized. After all, each analyst attracts a particular clientele of referring doctors, and within limits these refer, and he accepts, a particular type of patient. Some analysts like to work with psychotics, some with perverts, some take on highly abnormal characters, and some do not. Moreover, each analyst sees the same patient differently, not only in detail but in terms of the depth of the patient's pathology and the existence of specific character traits to which he may feel sympathetic or unsympathetic. If one has a patient who has previously been analysed by someone else, the differences in viewpoint are usually striking. The attention of two analysts may have floated evenly, but it has alighted at different points. In accounts of analyses, although analysts often describe their reactions to individual patients, their psychic work, as Widlöcher (1976) has pointed out, in general remains mysterious.

General attitudes also seem to characterize most psychoanalysts, or sometimes a particular school of psychoanalysts – the palaeo-Freudian emphasis on auto-erotism, the palaeo-Kleinian attempts to interpret the unconscious directly without paying attention to the defences, or the general conspiracy to ignore the traumatic effects of transference, to which I will return later.

First, however, I wish to discuss the idiosyncratic

ILLUSION AND
SPONTANEITY IN
PSYCHOANALYSIS

nature of the relationship of analyst and patient. Having criticized the loose use of the term countertransference, which ranges from a diagnosis of the analyst's psychopathology to the attribution to his unconscious of powers of assessment, in my last lecture (p. 29), I will start with the way in which what might be called true, normal countertransference reveals itself. It seems to me that the sign of countertransference lies in what the analyst habitually accepts from the patient and what he habitually ignores. In *The Language of Psycho-Analysis* (1973) Laplanche and Pontalis define countertransference, from their reading of the literature, as 'especially a response to the patient's transference'. I think that further definition is needed of the transference that we are responding to.

We do respond strongly to the patient's transference as it emanates in his atmosphere. For instance, what psychoanalyst has not been enmeshed in the sadistic power to control him which can be exercised by a patient of charm and intelligence? How difficult it is for an analyst with a boring patient to work with the patient on the problem of why he is so boring, rather than simply to be bored by him! But essentially the main part of what we call the patient's transference is an illusion from the past, and therefore essentially it misses its mark. The daily work of psychoanalysis consists in pointing this out by means of interpretation, and I am not convinced that our countertransference is, in its most significant aspect, a response to it. I think that our countertransference is essentially a response not to the patient's transference, but to his personality. That is to say, it is a transference which refuses to recognize the individuality of the patient because we project archaic images on to him. In our individual style of analysis, we continually resume our dispute with our own archaic internal objects.

It is time to take stock of where this is leading us: it is to a modification of the traditional view of the psychoanalytic interaction. The traditional view has been that the patient brings his fantasies in a way which is ultimately unmodified by the individual character of the analyst, or even by the analyst's sex; and that these fantasies stimulate reciprocal fantasies in the analyst, which can be a useful guide to the patient's psychological situation. While this view contains important elements of truth, it neglects the open-ended game between the habitual character of patient and analyst, which also has to be resolved. It neglects the interplay of *ethos* between analyst and patient, a word which originally meant the accustomed layer of an animal – from which, as all analysts know, we are able to emerge only with great difficulty.

Freud said early in his career that we can cure hysterical symptoms but not the hysterical character (Breuer and Freud, 1893–5, p. 39). I think that even today most analysts would agree that character problems are modifiable rather than curable, even though the modifications are often sufficient to make analysis worthwhile. This must apply in the analytic relationship too, and I believe that a *modus vivendi* is unconsciously found by means of the modelling myth referred to in my Inaugural Lecture (p. 11), which enables analyst and patient to do useful work together. This useful work must mean that both analyst and patient must, in some respects, and through their interaction, achieve the difficult task of some significant, if slight, modification in character. This possibility of change, I think, is what gives the psychoanalytic career its longterm attraction for the psychoanalyst, and also what imposes the strain on him.

Psychoanalysis is in fact a self-analysis for both patient and analyst, a self-analysis which today must take both the traditional view of psychoanalysis and newer views into account. (If analysis consisted only of interpreting the interplay of character, it would not differ much from counselling.) The projection of early-developed unconscious fantasy in the transference and the analysis of it are fundamental to the elucidation of the meaning of symptoms, which can only occur in terms of infantile sexuality and aggression. But if analysis explained symptoms only in terms of infantile sexuality, it would look antiquated and one-sided. The area of analysis which

requires most skill, and most mental acuity and control
– as well as intuition – is that in which these primitively
based symptoms are expressed in terms of the interpersonal relationship with the analyst. This is where the
fantasies which are condensed in the symptom are
covertly expressed in the preconceptions of the relationship. I had better give an example

A woman suffered from a phobia of spiders. So intense
was her fear that she could scarcely look at the analyst in
case he turned out to be a spider. It gradually emerged
that she felt she should never have married her rich
husband, and that when she left him, she had good
grounds to fear what actually happened: that he would
gradually starve himself to death. She had therefore been
the spider who had lured her husband into her web and
devoured him. Similarly, although she felt that she had
been a good mother to her two children, she feared she
had tied both of them to her, and to each other, in a way
which seriously interfered with their capacity for sexual
love. All this was rooted in an early conception of sexual
intercourse as a destructive attack from an unknown
quarter, and an even earlier fantasy – or perhaps appreciation – of her mother's power to enslave her by seductive
rejection. Here was a patient who was clearly very ill,
sometimes hallucinating the analyst's voice from different
parts of the room, sometimes cowering from him and
expecting him to spring, not infrequently speaking of
suicide. The analyst felt that she could not be left for
the whole duration of his usual holidays, and he was
reinforced in this belief by the serious impulsive behaviour
that had ensued when he informed her at the first consultation that he would not be able to treat her for some
time, and recommended her to a colleague. Moreover, he
liked her. In spite of her disturbance, she was in many
ways considerate, crisply intelligent and not lacking in
humour. You will easily see that the analyst was well
caught in the spider's web, and that interpretation of both
infantile fantasy and current character attitudes was
necessary to extricate both from the entanglement.

IMPLIED
AND DENIED
CONCEPTS

This example is a simple one. The symptom was clear-cut and its re-enactment in the transference relationship could be elucidated without much logical difficulty, though with considerable emotional difficulty on each side in seeing what was happening. But where the symptom is less clear-cut, the elucidation of its re-enactment in the transference is likely to be more arbitrary. For instance, in some analyses the patient finds the interpretations difficult to understand. It may happen that such a patient recounts a history of an early feeding disturbance, and his language may be characterized by a great deal of oral metaphor. The analyst may become convinced that the early feeding disturbance is being re-enacted in relation to his interpretations, and interprets the patient's difficulty in understanding in these terms. But the patient may reply that the difficulty lies in the analyst's confusion and inability to use language properly. The patient's accusation may have some justification, but this would not dispose of a further interpretation: that his sensitivity to the analyst's confusion expresses his feeling as a baby that the difficulty was all his mother's fault, for not understanding his needs.

This situation could degenerate into a circular wrangle between analyst and patient, and occasionally this is what seems to happen. The complexity in the cause of such a relationship was well expressed unconsciously, by one patient, in her complaint, 'It was just like life with Father all over again.' But more often patient and analyst gradually work through the wrangle by seeing the other's point of view and by refining the accuracy and points of applicability of their mutual interpretations. These mutual interpretations are the substrate which stimulates the self-analysis of each. This is what in the patient begins, and in the analyst refreshes, the continued work of self-exploration, the path to 'the true last judgement' which Proust rightly found in a work of art. It is the work that brings patient and analyst together.

If we examine this bond in more detail, we can see that it consists of something more complex than is described by the psychoanalytic cliché 'positive transference'. Posi- tive it is, but certainly not crudely sexual, as the transference was originally thought to be – though the exclusively sexual concept of transference was much modified, in Freud's thought, with the introduction into it of projected images of the self and the superego. The amount of sexual transference that 'positive transference' must contain is certainly unquantifiable, though most analysts do not doubt that its origins are closely connected with the origins of love, and that these involve a physical bond. But the phrase is used not simply of emotions, rather of the whole personality. The implicit concepts on which we rely are far wider than can be subsumed under the libido theory, and we should attempt a finer definition of the elements of attachment, sympathy, sexuality, identification, 'working alliance' and many more in the relationship. Our ingrained belief in the ubiquity of the libido, true as it is, can blind us to the true psychological condition of the ego. Without being false it can limit our horizons.

Here I wish to return to a subject touched on in my last two lectures. I wish to draw attention to areas where I believe that our over-simplified views of transference and resistance blind us to a number of phenomena which interfere with the smooth progress of analysis, and even more with the resolution of transference after the analysis is over.

Resistance has classically been viewed as the counterpart in analysis of the phenomenon of repression. Impulses which led to a fantasied danger in childhood such as the fear of castration – itself a cliché word for the fear of loss of all parts of the genital apparatus – are repressed or, as was increasingly realized, especially in Anna Freud's *The Ego and the Mechanisms of Defence* (1936), otherwise warded off. The analyst's attempt to name such impulses by interpretation of their unconscious content is countered by a renewed attempt to ward them off, that is, it meets with the patient's resistance. All this

42 is basic to psychoanalysis. And although what I have to say is in a sense peripheral, and in some ways banal, I believe that it is still important to say it.

There are many other reasons, besides automatic defence against the unconscious, which account for resistance to interpretations. What sounds the most superficial – but in fact characterizes them all – is that the analyst might have got it wrong. That this is important is sometimes denied by psychoanalysts, and sometimes ignored. It is denied on the grounds that if an interpretation is wrong, this will soon be discovered through the internal evidence of the analysis, supplied either by the patient or the analyst. The patient's fear of a wrong interpretation is interpreted in the transference as his fear of being (say) poisoned, or castrated, or of having his personality taken from him in some other way. All these transferences, and many more, may be relevant. But what is also relevant – to take an example from a much less emotional sphere – is that the notes on a lecture taken by members of a highly intelligent audience, or even the minutes of a board meeting, often appear highly one-sided to the lecturer or to the members of the board. Thus what is neglected is the rational disquiet of the patient about the capacity of the analyst to work with him towards true and satisfying solutions of his complex problem. I believe that resistance is basically the counterpart of repression; but I also believe that a great deal of resistance is due to a suspicion of the analyst on the part of the patient which is not entirely unhealthy, and can be provoked by the analyst unnecessarily.

It is time to give another example. As I say this, I realize that I was thinking of one a minute ago. If I were reassured by an analyst that a wrong interpretation would be quickly detected, my suspicions would be aroused; and in fact the patient of whom I was thinking did take flight from the analyst several months later, with a feeling that something of importance would not be understood. Dogmatic certainty and over-confidence arouse resistance. Freud referred to this problem in 'Constructions in analysis' (1937b), indicating that there may be good reason for the patient's reservations and that analytic reconstructions of childhood can be partial only.

There are many other ways of stimulating resistance to communication on the part of the patient which do not indicate an unwillingness to listen on the part of the analyst. I would like to give an example of this which was very convincing to me at the time, but may not be so convincing when reported. An analyst was speaking about a patient who had a terrible history. The man and his sister were twins, and when they were three their father committed suicide. Six months later their mother died. The twins were separated, each being taken by a different relative. After a lot of difficulty the boy managed to get himself a university education and subsequently an analysis. After some eighteen months his analyst died, and he had to go to somebody new. During one of the first sessions the bell rang in the new analyst's flat. The analyst went to open the door and returned. The patient said, 'I was wondering whether you do analysis full-time or whether you do something else as well.' The analyst replied, 'You want to know what kind of a person I am.' As soon as I heard this I found my eyes meeting those of a colleague. We had both been chilled by the rebuffing quality of the remark to this severely deprived and frightened man.

What I am emphasizing is that the implicit concepts underlying the personality of the analyst can be important in diminishing the potency of his explicit concepts. Of course all analysts are aware of the importance of the personal factor but, as I have said, its systematic study remains a lacuna in psychoanalytic theory.

Its importance lies in the fact that it is the therapeutic aspects of the analyst's personality which counteract the inevitably traumatic effects of developing a transference. In my Inaugural Lecture (p. 4) I emphasized the therapeutic aspects of transference formation, but the formation of transference has its regressive aspects as well. To surrender oneself to thoughts which are normally held in repression is very frightening, and the flight from reality which regularly follows – that is, the development of the transference illusion – is testimony to it.

Of course transference also has to be developed for reasons which have little to do with trauma. No experience, as Proust emphasized so insistently, can be reached effectively by memory alone, only by the association of memory with sensations in the present. Therefore the recapture of past time must necessarily be interpenetrated with a present situation. Swann could not remember being in love with Odette when he thought about it, but the experience was brought back to him with all its pain by a phrase of Vinteuil's sonata.

The development of transference is, none the less, truly a trauma, traumatic experience being defined by Freud as one in which the ego is rendered helpless in the face of excessive excitation, whether of external or internal origin (1926). The excitation in the face of which the ego regresses in psychoanalysis is of course the breach of the barrier of repression, which exposes the patient to his involuntary and previously unconscious thoughts. The regression results in a dependency on the part of the patient which can make the effect of absence, whether through holidays, illness or cancellation a prime source of disturbance to the patient and of concern to the analyst. It is a dependency which can change to hostility on the part of the patient after the analysis is over. It is a dependency which may be lifelong, especially on the part of analysts who have difficulty in overcoming the ambivalent attachment to their training analyst which working together as colleagues makes difficult to break.

However helpful the experience of analysis may be, its results in the relationship are always infantilizing. This the patient must resent, whether he does so consciously or not, and it poses a serious technical problem to be solved. The counterpart of this is that at present the therapeutic effects of analysis must rely on aspects of the analyst's personality which are able to neutralize the persecutory quality inherent in the formation of transfer-

ence. It is here that the analyst's ability to listen, not to
be dogmatic, and to be spontaneous – which means to be
sincere – are all important.

It is a difficult task for the analyst. If he is to be an
effective psychoanalyst, and at the same time completely
sincere, he will need to have the genius of Freud. If he is
to borrow what he has learnt from Freud, or from Melanie
Klein, or from some other pioneer, he becomes a disciple
rather than a pupil, according to the distance by which
his transference makes him feel that his teacher excels
him. Becoming a pupil or a disciple must inevitably
interfere with his spontaneity and must cause him conflict
in his search for the inner truth, the expression of which
will form 'the true last judgement' of him by his patient.
Nietzsche's remarks about disciples are relevant: 'There
was only one Christian and he died on the Cross' (1888,
p. 178). There was, I think, only one Freudian, who, in
spite of a basic consistency, was free enough to change
his mind quite a lot during his life. His thought was
revolutionary, and he needed disciples for his ideas to
prevail, and I think he still does. But discipleship brings
terrible problems. And non-discipleship in psychoanalysis brings even worse problems. It is a hard life for the
analyst, and the analyst should not recommend psychoanalysis too lightly for the patient.

IMPLIED
AND DENIED
CONCEPTS

5 JOHN KLAUBER –
INDEPENDENT CLINICIAN

Neville Symington

JOHN KLAUBER was due to assume the Freud Memorial Visiting Professorship at University College London when, just six weeks before his Inaugural Lecture, he died unexpectedly on 11 August 1981. He had completed the first four lectures which he intended to give, and the fifth one was half-finished. The Inaugural Lecture was presented at University College by his colleague, Dr Eric Rayner, who also read it some two months later to an audience at the British Psycho-Analytical Society.

Many of those who heard this lecture spontaneously recognized that John Klauber had opened a new vista of understanding within psychoanalysis. Whereas psycho-analytic understanding had been underpinned by a basic assumption that cure was effected through bringing the patient to a stage where he or she was able to make judgements about reality unclouded by illusory or delusional elements, John Klauber boldly stated that this end was only achievable through the agency of illusion. He pointed out that the transference, which is central to

ILLUSION AND
SPONTANEITY IN
PSYCHOANALYSIS

psychoanalysis, was a dramatization of the patient's illusions and that the analyst set a stage to enable this to occur. As soon as he had said this its truth was staringly obvious to all analysts but, like so many important truths, it was so transparent that it had not been seen.

Reality, of course, cannot be apprehended directly. Man can grasp the *noumenon* through an act of the intellect, but his experience of reality in all its variegated aspects is only possible indirectly; it is the *phenomenon* that the individual man or woman knows. This distinction has been clear to psychologists and philosophers since Kant first elaborated it in the *Critique of Pure Reason* (1781). It is through illusion that man comprehends reality. If man grasps reality through the agency of illusion, then distortion or misperception must imply that this agency is faulty in some way. John Klauber's formulation can therefore be seen as an attempt to bring the goals of psychoanalysis within an accepted spectrum of philosophical and psychological understanding. It is a viewpoint heralded in a startling statement by Hippolyte Taine:

External perception is an internal dream which proves to be in harmony with external things; and instead of calling hallucination a false external perception, we must call external perception a true *hallucination.* (quoted in Reeves, p. 104)

John Klauber's Inaugural Lecture then suggests that psychoanalysis enables the patient to correct flaws in his or her internal dream or illusion via which reality is perceived. However, the approach is not just valuable because it brings psychoanalysis into harmony with philosophical thinking, but also because it lays stress on the value of the patient's illusions. Whereas illusion has been perceived negatively – by analysts who have thought it to be a factor which sabotages the analytic endeavour – John Klauber focused on its positive value. This positive attitude underlay all Klauber's thinking: in his analytic work he created an ethos that favoured the development of the positive factors within the personality.

Because this first lecture of Klauber's has been recognized as an important contribution to psychoanalytic thinking it has been thought worthwhile to publish the lectures in book form as he had written them. Four of the lectures are complete, though no doubt he would have modified them here and there. The fifth, half-finished lecture is not being published. As a background to these lectures I intend to indicate what I believe was Klauber's unique contribution.

John Klauber demythologized psychoanalysis, and did this from several angles. Let me start with the idea that the patient knows nothing about the analyst. I do not know quite when this idea was introduced into psychoanalytic discussion; all Freud's analysands knew a good deal about him, so it is an idea that has entered analytic thinking later. John Klauber believed that patients always knew quite a lot about the analyst and said so explicitly.

When the patient visits the psychoanalyst for a consultation, it is not only the psychoanalyst who makes an assessment of the patient – the patient also attempts to make an assessment of the analyst. Though the transference, which begins to be formed before the consultation, has an important share in the patient's subsequent reaction, the capacity of the patient's ego to evaluate it is not paralysed, as later analysis tends to reveal. Just as a psychoanalyst starts his report on a patient by describing what he looks like, how he moves and how he is dressed, so equally a fund of information about the psychoanalyst reaches the patient about his capacity to respond, about his tastes and personal attitudes, as displayed, for instance, by the pictures on his walls. Some psychoanalysts seem to regard this as unfortunate and attempt to limit its effectiveness by establishing a so-called 'neutral' setting. I believe that the second attitude fails to give adequate credit to human intelligence and the human unconscious. A woman, undoubtedly suffering from paranoid tendencies, gave as her grounds for refusing treatment with a particular psychoanalyst that she could never be analysed by someone who decorated his consulting room with such bad art. The patient herself had a considerable sensitivity for the visual arts, which she had demonstrated by discerning purchases. One psychoanalyst reported this decision as the arch evidence for the unreasonableness of the patient. A second thought that the perceptiveness which marked her character, perhaps in some respects sharpened by her paranoid tendencies, had made her quickly understand that a psychoanalyst with such taste in pictures would only with great difficulty acquire a sufficient affinity with her own personality to understand it. (1981, pp. 129–30)

Klauber believed that the transference was such a powerful emotional phenomenon that it was not necessary to set up a neutral setting, even supposing that this were possible, because it weaved itself around the setting which was there. A small example might illustrate this point. One morning a patient saw me reading the newspaper through the window before he came into the consulting room. When he started to talk he said he thought I was reading the notes which I had made about him after his last session; he thought I was anxious about him, and awaiting his arrival eagerly. I was again reading the paper before the next patient came. He had seen me reading the newspaper, and thought I must have sighed within myself as I saw him coming and wished I could have gone on reading it.

In the passage from *Difficulties in the Analytic Encounter* quoted above there is ground for believing that the second analyst was John Klauber himself, for Klauber did not think that all interpersonal difficulties could be analysed. Indeed the idea that everything could be analysed was a myth: the analyst's own capacities are limited and there is no analyst without blind spots. (I think most of us have quite blatant ones.) John Klauber

JOHN KLAUBER–
INDEPENDENT
CLINICIAN

50 constantly challenged the idea that perfection could be
    attained. He recognized that there is a deep yearning in
    mankind for perfection; he also knew that this striving
    after perfection was necessary. For it is a paradox that
    man needs the goal of perfection if he is to triumph over
    those obstacles that stand in the way of the establishment
    of humane attitudes towards others, both within the
    individual and society at large. Man needs this goal, yet
    at the same time also needs to know that the goal is not
    attainable. It was this latter dimension of the paradox
    that John Klauber stressed. If it is really believed that
    perfection can be achieved then it leads to the legitimation
    of tyranny, sadism and persecution. Klauber thought that
    if it were really believed that psychoanalytic ideals were
    attainable, it would provide licence for cruelty. In his
    paper 'Personal attitudes to psychoanalytic consultation'
    (1981, pp. 141–59), he says,

> The quicker the patient is put at his ease, the freer the
> communication and the fuller the consultation. This also
> is obvious, and I would not stress it unless I believed that
> the ethos of the detached analyst – or the analyst as a
> mirror – were sometimes used as a cover for sadism. (p.
> 149)

It was similar thinking which led him to say that therapeutic change did not occur through transference interpretations alone. Here he challenged the view which had
been pioneered by James Strachey (1934) and had been
widely followed, certainly within the British Psycho-
Analytical Society. When he gave his paper on this subject
to the British Society, 'Formulating interpretations in
clinical psychoanalysis' (1981, pp. 109–20), his viewpoint was firmly criticized by the main discussant. Truth
can never be the possession of any isolated element, and
John Klauber, believing that truth was the agent of the
psychoanalytic cure, said so on various occasions. In 'The
relationship of transference and interpretation' (1981,
pp. 25–43), he says, 'The human mind is satisfied, and in
some sense healed, by what it feels as truth' (p. 36).

Truth is a flighty lady and will never allow any one idea, person, group of persons, ideology, religion or school to possess her. As soon as she sees the tentacles of the octopus she flees from sight. It is clear from John Klauber's writings that, as I have said, he did not consider therapeutic change to occur through interpretations alone. Similarly, he did not think that the strict analytic stance could always be maintained. It was the ideal, but there were patients for whom it was too great a stress to their egos, as he says in his paper 'A particular form of transference in neurotic depression' (1981, pp. 91–108). After talking about a patient whom others might call borderline, he says:

The lunchtime analytic hour we had agreed upon reduced the much-needed time available for her work. It was necessary eventually to recognize the impossibility of her ego's mediating her demands – and that the analyst could be capable of making an unsuitable arrangement – and I gave her a time which would both enable her to come late (as she always did) and to have extra time at the end . . .

It may seem contradictory that a modification of standard technique should be advocated after previously emphasizing the danger of being seduced by the depressive patient's dependency. But such an acceptance of her need at this phase of the analysis enabled guilt and aggression which had been mobilized to be recognized instead of projected: first, it reduced the disruption due to the burden of her realistic anxiety; second, it showed that I did not consider myself infallible, but was prepared to listen to her in spite of her abuse. All this paved the way for the interpretation of her fantasy that she had killed her father by her unawareness of his need. In my opinion a technique which recognizes the urgency of the patient's psychic and realistic predicament is to be distinguished from a technique of encouragement at the beginning of analysis. The latter impedes the isolation of the patient's real difficulties. (pp. 104–5)

I think John Klauber always kept in mind that ideals were

JOHN KLAUBER-
INDEPENDENT
CLINICIAN

not fully attainable. This did not imply a lack of striving or enthusiasm, but rather a constant recognition that disappointment was one of the growing pains in the struggle for maturity. He knew that tragedy lay at the heart of human existence; he believed that fanaticism and the idea that perfection was attainable were defences against disappointment. Some years ago in America, for example, there was a sect who believed that the end of the world was due to happen on a particular date. When the day arrived the members of the sect climbed up a mountain and waited for the end of the world to occur. When the expected event did not happen what did the members of the sect do? Abandon their belief? No, they recalculated the date from the relevant biblical passages and went off and proselytized with a renewed fervour. Klauber thought that the proclamation of the Resurrection of Christ and the new enthusiasm of Pentecost were manic defences on the part of the apostles of Jesus in the face of a shattering disappointment when their hero was crucified. By analysing early disappointment he helped patients to face this imperfect world and to face their own diminishments. He certainly had a pessimistic view of the human scene but it was coupled with great joy and contentment in living. He had integrated disappointment, which I believe is a rare human achievement, and had no feeling that life had cheated or betrayed him.

Klauber knew that the patient should ideally tell the analyst everything; but again he knew that this goal was not attainable. In his paper entitled 'The relationship of transference and interpretation', he says that

One thing is certain; no patient tells or can tell his analyst everything, even of what consciously occurs to him. Every patient keeps his secrets, whether from a desire to keep an area of his life unanalysed, to convince himself of his own power to contain his deepest fears, or because he fears to hurt the analyst excessively. But whatever his motive, it implies a considerable area of reserve. (1981, p. 53)

Klauber did not think it was possible for any analyst to
hold a neutral stance in relation to his patients, or even
in relation to particular aspects of a patient's character
as it manifested itself to him in the consulting room. The
analyst's own values are mobilized by the situations which
the patient brings. Some analysts might see smoking as
the manifestation of a destructive impulse and direct interpretations accordingly, while others may think that it
manifests a capacity to use pleasure to adapt to particular
life conditions. Klauber has this to say.

*The individual (psychoanalyst or patient) prizes and tries
to preserve his value systems because they reflect the
attempts at adjustment of the ego and ego ideal to those
compromises formed between drive and primitive defence
which have acquired permanent structure. Such ideals
may take forms compatible or incompatible with the
ideals of individual psychoanalysts: propensities towards
austerity or luxury, towards the acceptance or non-
acceptance of commonly held standards of choice of
work, or even of dress, which may be treated by one
psychoanalyst as symptoms and by another with toler-
ation. An example might be the longing of a successful
academic to become a painter. The choice of each career
was determined by ambivalent identifications. It might
be maintained that the development of the patient's
personality through systematic analysis would ultimately
decide the choice of career. But the use of the word*
ultimately *would suggest a denial of the importance of
what happens in the meantime. In practice it is difficult
for the psychoanalyst, when confronted with the immi-
nence of a decisive choice by the patient, not to find that
his own system of values inevitably comes into operation.
For example, a woman suffering from sexual inhibition
was married to a successful husband who suffered from
severe unreliability of his character. The result of her first
analysis in another country was to give her greater
freedom of sexual expression, but she could obtain no
satisfaction from her husband, and she started a liaison*

JOHN KLAUBER–
INDEPENDENT
CLINICIAN

54　*with a man of lower social class. The first psychoanalyst's interpretations were directed towards stopping the liaison, which was rightly regarded as an acting out of transference fantasies. At this stage it became necessary for the husband's career that the couple should move to England. The patient began a second analysis and commented early that the second analyst's view of the liaison was quite different from that of the first. While he agreed that it expressed transference fantasies, his interpretations acknowledged the increase in the ego's capacity for decision which had accompanied the liberation of her sexuality and sympathized with her need for sexual fulfilment.* (1981, pp. 131–2)

This is consistent with John Klauber's view that the selection of interpretations is conditioned by the analyst's own value system. For Klauber values did not just exist in the superego part of the personality, but conditioned qualitative factors in the ego and id as well. He makes this surprising statement in one of his papers:

Values are the individual's encoded judgements of the successful co-operation in the past between the three psychic structures, and they become the preconditions without which drive satisfaction is reduced or rendered impossible. (p. 115)

In other words, a person's character cannot be separated from the value system in which he or she was brought up. The judgements that a person makes determine the way he or she is in the future, and judgements condition the impulse life of the id. This means that attitudes which are the product of established values determine the selection of interpretations, and that the decision on which interpretative line to select will be determined in important ways by the analyst's individual values. It is frustrating, however, that Klauber does not take this further, because it seems an inevitable conclusion that the kind of person whom the patient meets becomes in itself an agent for change or otherwise in psychoanalysis. He probably rightly wanted to steer away from this and try instead to examine more fully the analytic process, which is in constant movement.

Klauber thought, therefore, that it was not possible for there to be an analysis with no collusions, and he preferred to have them in the open. If he came across a patient who had a love of wine like himself and the patient perceived it, he preferred to acknowledge it and let it be something which individualized that particular analysis.

Of course John Klauber recognized that the analytic technique with its associated myths had evolved for a purpose. He was aware that an intimate situation where strong emotions were aroused could be difficult to contain; to maintain a professional stance is not easy. It was for this reason that he constantly drew attention to the burdensome nature of the analyst's work, and he once said that he could think of no other profession that was as stressful. Thus Klauber did not condemn an analyst because he geared some interpretations to protect himself. What he wanted was honesty about it. If the analyst was truthful with himself about it, even if it was not verbalized, this fact in itself was therapeutic. It is working in the presence of truth that heals.

I think perhaps the most revolutionary paper of Klauber's was the one entitled 'Elements of the psychoanalytic relationship and their therapeutic implications' (1981, pp. 45–62). In the helping professions there is considerable expression of contempt for the worker who needs his or her patients or clients; Klauber, facing this squarely, says that the analyst needs the patient, and then defines what the analyst needs his patients for. I quote from a passage which I think is perhaps the most remarkable thing he ever wrote:

Patient and analyst need one another. The patient comes to the analyst because of internal conflicts that prevent him from enjoying life, and he begins to use the analyst not only to resolve them, but increasingly as a receptacle for his pent-up feelings. But the analyst also needs the

JOHN KLAUBER–
INDEPENDENT
CLINICIAN

patient in order to crystallize and communicate his own thoughts, including some of his inmost thoughts on intimate human problems which can only grow organically in the context of this relationship. They cannot be shared and experienced in the same immediate way with a colleague, or even with a husband or wife. It is also in his relationship with his patients that the analyst refreshes his own analysis. It is from this mutual participation in analytic understanding that the patient derives the substantial part of his cure and the analyst his deepest confidence and satisfaction. (p. 46)

Several points in this passage are worth our dallying over a while. Here Klauber sees analysis as a servant of a deeper purpose: the need to find answers to deep human questions. This is not detached research but something that is necessary for psychic health. For example, some have solved their inner anguish and questioning through writing. In the first volume of his autobiography, *A Sort of Life* (1971), Graham Greene says that he wrote in order to make some sense out of the chaos of human experience. Similarly Somerset Maugham, in *Cakes and Ale* (1930, p. 202), says that an author exorcizes deep grief through writing about it. D. H. Lawrence said that art was not for art's sake but his own sake, and Klauber's first sentence in *Difficulties in the Analytic Encounter* is in the same vein: 'What one writes is primarily for oneself' (p. xiii).

The analyst's artistic medium is in his daily interpretative work with his patients. Psychoanalysis, for the analyst, becomes the medium of a deeper purpose and one that he shares with the artist, writer, philosopher, poet and musician. For Klauber, psychoanalysis was ever a means and not an end. 'Psychoanalysis is made for man, not man for psychoanalysis,' he once said, misquoting Christ's famous dictum about the Sabbath. The value of psychoanalytic research was to illuminate problematic areas in wider spheres of human living. It was something George Eliot expressed when she wrote of

that agreeable after-glow of excitement when thought
lapses from examination of a specific object into a
suffusive sense of its connections with all the rest of our
existence. (1871–2, p. 194)

From what I have said so far it might be concluded that
John Klauber considered psychoanalysis a subjective art
that depended, for the most part, on the skill and integrity
of the individual analyst alone. However, this was not his
position and in fact he believed that psychoanalysis was
a science, in 1968 writing a paper on the subject entitled
'On the dual use of historical and scientific method in
psychoanalysis' (1981, pp. 181–204). In this paper he
makes it clear that he believes psychoanalysis, although
not a natural science, to be a science because it aims to
provide a single explanatory schema for a multiplicity of
phenomena. Yet the Freud Memorial lectures seem to
indicate that he doubted the validity of trying to make
out that psychoanalysis is a science!

The effort to make psychoanalysis into a science has
tended to play down the importance of the individual
personality of the analyst in spite of the fact that the
analyst's personality is clearly central to the technique.
(this volume, p. 35)

The conclusion seems to be that the scientific model is
deficient. Now it is of course true that no model can ever
match the clinical reality, but Klauber is not making that
general point here. He says specifically that *the effort*
to make psychoanalysis into a science plays down the
importance of the analyst's personality and is therefore
deficient. He must therefore implicitly be criticizing the
scientific model that most analysts function with. Did he
intend to pose some new theoretical model in later
lectures? As Klauber was a man with considerable self-
knowledge, it is difficult not to think that he had realized
the implication of his remarks. My guess is that he would
probably not have done so in this series of lectures, but
would probably have indicated that it was a necessary

next step for someone to take. Had he lived he might have made the attempt later.

John Klauber said once that most of the ideas he had written about had been fairly clear in his mind soon after qualifying as an analyst. He was a cautious man, and he let an idea mature for a long time before he committed it to paper. Even if he disagreed with another's point of view he usually respected it, and if there was a big body of opinion against what he, Klauber, thought his respect was even greater. He would have been very wary of challenging a view which was held by the majority. He would have had even greater reserve about criticizing Freud in any major way.

So these lectures are within the framework of traditional Freudian theory, but the implications of them point in quite a revolutionary direction. What is certain is that Klauber's clinical way of working diverged a long way from the current theories and from the technical methods based upon them. He had the courage to depart from the technique accepted and followed by the majority of analysts. In a rare moment he once admitted that most of his patients got better, and it is for this reason that he deserves to be listened to with a keen ear. All of us need to look at the signposts which he was creating, and I think if we are to do him justice we need to reconsider the theories which we implicitly accept. In the future, when analysts look back to the careful observations that he made, and to their implications, John Klauber may be recognized as the prophet of a renewal within psychoanalysis. This is particularly clear in the importance which he placed upon interpretation.

John Klauber said explicitly that interpretation was not the prime agent of change in psychoanalysis. 'The analyst's first job,' he said, 'is to make emotional contact with his patient.' In many a clinical presentation an analyst will be heard to say to his colleagues: 'I made

contact with the patient at the beginning of the session but then he drifted off.' 'I became aware that I was no longer in contact with the patient.' 'Although the patient had been acting out I managed to stay in contact.' Similarly we will often hear statements such as these in a clinical presentation: 'I interpreted the patient's covert hostility and he assented, yet I knew I was missing the point.' 'Although I was making interpretations which seemed to be accurate, yet the whole atmosphere was false and gave me the feeling that it was all a charade.' 'Despite good interpretative work I sensed that an underlying level was not being reached.'

We know this as analysts; and yet we seem to insist that making interpretations is the analyst's most important function, while knowing that it is to make emotional contact with our patients. Why then do we not say so explicitly and make it clear that interpretation is secondary? I want to trace through some of Klauber's lines of thinking and see if, by doing so, we get some more light thrown on to this difficult question.

Klauber did make emotional contact with his patients and they did get better. I don't think it is possible to say how he made emotional contact, but I think it is possible to delineate an array of factors which he believed favoured its occurrence.

What most commonly blocked emotional contact, Klauber believed, was the analyst's own anxieties. He therefore thought that someone training to be an analyst needed to undergo a searching analysis, and should try to resolve his or her most deep-seated problems. Klauber thought that envy, pathological jealousy, sexual perversion and paranoia had their roots in an area of the personality variously named by different authors: the schizoid level by Fairbairn, the basic fault by Balint, the pre-oedipal, pregenital area or area of psychotic anxieties by Melanie Klein and her school. He had the idea that if emotional contact was made here then the patient became healed, and that if the analyst was healed at this deep level he or she would be able to pass it on to his or her patients. If this was done then the envy, jealousy and sexual perversion could, as it were, look after themselves.

JOHN KLAUBER–
INDEPENDENT
CLINICIAN

Thus he was against the approach of those analysts who believed that the minutiae of the transference needed to be analysed in detail. I sympathize with the generosity of attitude behind this recommendation, but know that certain patients will manage to avoid the analytic process unless there is a detailed following of their communications to the analyst.

When extensive emotional contact had been made with this psychotic area of the personality, Klauber believed, it was probably time for the analysis to end. His ideas about the time needed for a thorough analysis were definite, though not rigid: four to five years was not long enough to allow a deep-enough contact with the psychotic area of the personality; to go beyond nine years, on the other hand, showed insufficient trust in the process. He also thought that the patient could not become an individual until the analysis had been at an end for some years. For when emotional contact is made and strong negative feelings have been 'worked through', the patient often has a high regard for his or her analyst and sometimes sees him or her as a sort of 'saviour'. The analyst then becomes a model of enormous influence for the patient, and it is very difficult for him or her to disengage from the analyst's aura and become an individual person.

For Klauber the aim of analysis was to set free the inner process of analysis, and it was his trust in this process that led him to distrust very long analyses; I think he saw the place of interpretation in this context. What the patient seeks is an object relationship, but through interpretation this desire is frustrated. Instead the patient receives understanding and a relationship based on identification rather than an object relationship. Mature object relationships within the maelstrom of life is what psychoanalysis aims to bring about. So the analyst as a gratifying object for the patient needs to be curtailed, as does the patient as a gratifying object for the analyst.

Interpretation, therefore, is a factor which puts boundaries within the analytic relationship and defines its role. Psychoanalysis could not happen without it, but it is not

what makes an analysis. It is like a man who buys some
land on which to build a house. The land has boundaries
to it, and he could not buy land that did not; but what is
essential for him in order to build his house is to have the
land itself on which the house can be founded. So also it
is emotional contact that an analysis is founded on, but
interpretations are its boundaries.

Moreover, you cannot tell a trainee how to make
emotional contact. One might imagine a scenario where
a trainee asks the experienced analyst how to make
contact with Joseph, his patient. The analyst explains to
the trainee what to say and do, and the trainee's eyes light
up with a flash of understanding; and away he goes and
it seems to work with Joseph, but then he tries it with
Mary and it seems to make her worse, so he rushes off to
another supervisor who says, 'Say this to Mary' and, what
a marvel, it works a treat; so then he tries it out on Tom,
and Tom goes into a catastrophic depression and leaves
analysis altogether and takes to drink into the bargain. I
think you see my point. The making of emotional contact
comes from only one place: at the creative centre of the
individual person. For this reason Klauber emphasized
spontaneity. Spontaneity – to be distinguished from
impulsiveness – springs from the ego in a state of freedom
from the superego and id; whereas impulsiveness comes
from the id. (Of course to say that spontaneity is an
essential concomitant for the role of analysis is an appal-
ling stumbling-block for any committee involved in
student training, because by very definition it is something
totally outside a committee's control; something which
it cannot legislate for. What a scandal for a committee
whose self-esteem is so bound up with laying down rules
for others!)

Spontaneity is an essential quality in an analyst, and
Klauber mentions that sometimes, as he was beginning
to speak an interpretation, another one interposed itself.
He would recommend following the one that sprang to
mind at the last moment. Indeed the very act of speaking
can sometimes evoke an insight in the analyst's mind, and

JOHN KLAUBER–
INDEPENDENT
CLINICIAN

it was for this reason that Klauber believed in talking more freely to the patient than would be customary within a classical analysis. He also thought, following Ferenczi, that if the analyst remained too detached he frequently repeated an original trauma – that of a child with a very distant parent. If the analyst did this he would be 'acting in' and taking on the role of the parent in the original trauma.

The beginning of an analysis was a trauma for the patient, Klauber thought, and the analyst detraumatized the patient through interpreting, and enabling him or her to make partial identifications with the analyst. He believed in spontaneity in the analyst and the maximum self-expression possible in the patient. It will sometimes happen, for instance, that a patient, having made a developmental move, will feel angry and hostile to those to whom he or she has been enslaved, and also display an omnipotent extravagance arising from a new-found freedom. Klauber believed that it was better to let this self-expression run its course than to jump on it, thinking thereby that the omnipotence became better integrated within the personality.

He was also thoroughly against forcing his viewpoint upon a patient, and did not think that he necessarily knew what was the best way to live a life. On one occasion a young analyst had started to see a patient who had had therapy beforehand on several occasions. The patient's history showed that it was likely he would not stay in treatment for very long. The analyst said, 'He is not taking his treatment seriously,' and Klauber replied, 'He will probably leave treatment, come back to it, leave it again.' The young analyst said, 'But don't you think that is the wrong attitude?' Klauber replied, 'It's his life, not yours.'

It is in this context of spontaneity and freedom that the deepest emotional contact takes place because it opens up the area of reverie in the analyst, while the patient stimulates it through his own free expression. Rigidity is always a defence against a psychotic area within the personality, and means that this area is not available for making contact with the patient. Freud recommended 'free-floating attention', Bion recommended the state of 'reverie'; and Klauber recommended spontaneity, which is the expression of the content of free-floating attention or reverie. Indeed spontaneity was so important to Klauber that he thought it better for the analyst to give expression to things than to hold back. This led him to speak to his patients more than was necessary, and about quite a number of topics that were not strictly necessary. It did sometimes interfere with the continuity of the analytic momentum. In this way he also reacted too much to the patient's non-verbal activation of the analyst, rather than bearing it and then analysing it; he extended the frame necessary for spontaneity too far.

To make emotional contact with the patient it is necessary to be as undefensive as possible. If a patient correctly intuited something about the analyst, John Klauber believed in acknowledging it, and he thought this helped to mend the split in the patient's mind between the analyst of fantasy and the real analyst. If challenged that by his tone of voice he seemed to betray a prejudice, he would own up to it – in this way a patient could feel that his attacks could really be sustained by the analyst. (It is so often clear from presentations that analysts are not able to manage annihilating attacks from their patients, especially when they come in the form of powerful projective identification.) This lack of defensiveness, so essential if emotional contact is to be made, can allow the analyst to be 'with' the patient. The patient feels that mutuality is at work and this strengthens his own ego and increases his self-esteem.

Of course Klauber believed that interpretations were crucial: they consolidated the process and laid down within the personality a foundation that would be there for good. Once insight has occurred the personality is structured differently, and the previous state of affairs cannot be returned to; but interpretations only had any true meaning and were only effective, he thought, if they

JOHN KLAUBER–
INDEPENDENT
CLINICIAN

64   were emotionally an expression of an achieved state of affairs.

Now the question is why did Klauber not devise a theory to frame his conceptualizations? He was critical of the received theory and technique, thinking it too reductionist. It did not give sufficient account of the personal elements in the bond between analyst and patient, and the centrality of emotional contact did not have a proper place theoretically. So why did he not forge a new theory? The answer to this question must lie in some element in his personality.

In every individual there is a struggle between the individual and the collective within, as Jung emphasized. John Klauber felt that he could be spontaneous with safety, as long as he respected the society of which he was a part, and its voice within him. He was very conscious of these two sides of him and gave expression to them on a variety of occasions. He believed deeply in the importance of listening to the inner light, and said on one occasion that he thought those who had had a Quaker upbringing had the potential to be good psychotherapists; on the other hand, he had a reverence for the group, the collective. This was manifested in his exaggerated reverence for the genius of Freud. (For example, he did not like Ellenberger's book on the unconscious (1970) because he thought it unfairly demoted Freud.)

Klauber knew himself well, which means that he knew his limitations. He was dissatisfied with the theory, and the technique which was closely wedded to it; he criticized the theory vigorously, but it seems that he was wary of trying to change it. He was prepared to take up his own personal approach to patients and justify his stance, but was not prepared to propose a new theory. Or perhaps he was not willing to found a new school of theory within psychoanalysis. In this he was like Ferenczi, whom he admired, and also like Balint and Winnicott. Thus he was the epitome of the Independent Group of analysts within the British Society, whose members are against the founding of schools.

Freud felt betrayed when Jung took issue with one of
the central tenets of his theory; in a similar way Melanie
Klein felt betrayed by Paula Heimann. It can only mean
that a theory is felt as one's creation and to have it
criticized is a personal attack. They felt as sensitive about
it as Michelangelo was when one of the cardinals criticized
his nude figures in the judgement scene in the Sistine
Chapel. There is, however, an added element in that both
Freud and Melanie Klein wanted the mental attitude of
their followers to be moulded according to their own
conceptualizations. Now perhaps we can see something
of Klauber's dilemma. If he becomes a forger of new
theory he goes against one of his own deepest principles:
that it is a *good* for individuals to find their own free
personal expression. With such a view how can you want
to forge others into your own image and likeness? That
is the dilemma of the person who espouses freedom in a
deep way. That was Klauber's dilemma, as it has been the
dilemma of those who believe in personal freedom. Isaiah
Berlin, in *Against the Current* (1979), instances some of
the few brave figures within the European tradition of
ideas who have set themselves against the great mono-
causal systems of thought: Vico, Herder, Montesquieu
and a few others – but their names will never be as famous
as Descartes, Karl Marx or Freud.

It seems then that to be individually wedded to freedom
may mean 'living within the shadow of a genius'; that it
is necessary to be a follower in order to have an internal
and interpersonal life, because to be the moulder of the
lives of others is intolerable for one who believes in
freedom. But this leaves a wound at the centre of a
person's being. Rousseau felt this dilemma when he said
in exasperation that men must be forced to be free. But I
think it may be that it is those who have felt this wound
at the centre of their being who have the capacity to heal.
Klauber was a very good healer. I think he would have
been satisfied with that epitaph.

JOHN KLAUBER–
INDEPENDENT
CLINICIAN

6 PSYCHOANALYSIS AND FREEDOM OF THE WILL

Roger Kennedy

I THINK that my former analyst, John Klauber, would have been interested in the subject matter of this paper, as he thought deeply on the problem of freedom in the analytic relationship. Although he was mainly concerned, in his writings, with the clinical problems encountered by analyst and analysand, he was always interested in the relevance of analysis to other disciplines, as well as the way in which the analyst needs to question basic analytic assumptions with the aid of other modes of thought, such as history or philosophy.

I wish to discuss the relationship between freedom of the will and psychoanalytic understanding. For although the topic of freedom of the will has been debated for centuries, I think that specific questions are concerned with the psychoanalytic contribution to the debate. Such questions arise from the analytic treatment setting – with the use of the couch to curb the analysand's ability to act; the expectation of the analysand's 'free associations'; and the search for the meaning of the analysand's communications. One could perhaps summarize the relevant ques-

tions in the following way. Although I have listed the
questions I shall not discuss each of them in turn in a
rigorous fashion as they are interlinked, and I do not
think they can be meaningfully discussed as discrete
entities.

1. How much freedom does the analysand have in undergoing psychoanalysis, and what are the specific curbs, if any, to his freedom?
2. How much choice does the analysand have about what is happening to him?
3. How does the analyst interfere with or, on the contrary, facilitate the analysand's freedom?
4. What are the acceptable limits, if any, to the analysand's freedom?
5. With what kind of freedom is the analyst dealing? And how can it be used for therapeutic purposes?
6. What is determined, and what is not determined, in the analytic situation?
7. Is the concept of freedom of the will necessary for psychoanalysis?
8. Are there underlying assumptions about the nature of freedom of the will inherent in current psychoanalytic knowledge? And,
9. Can psychoanalysis make a significant contribution to our understanding of the nature of freedom of the will?

I shall attempt to discuss some of these questions, but there are inevitably no complete answers. First of all, one should perhaps begin by stating that it is difficult to define what is meant by freedom of the will, and what is meant by 'freedom', as definitions have been constantly evolving. Views as to the existence or non-existence of the will, freedom, and freedom of the will seem to be in a constant state of flux. One could say, following A. J. Ayer (1954, p. 15), that 'When I am said to have done something of my own free will it is implied that I could have acted otherwise; and it is only when it is believed that I could have acted otherwise that I am held morally responsible for what I have done.' From this definition it follows that

68   the human subject can only feel remorse, a sense of
being responsible for actions, when he could have acted
otherwise. There are, however, times when a free moral
agent can only do *one* thing, as with Luther's 'Here I
stand, I can do no other.' There are also times, as with a
suicidal patient, when the idea of doing only one thing,
i.e., commit suicide, is evidence of a loss of freedom and
of hope.

St Thomas Aquinas's definition of free will is another
useful reference point, as many later definitions of free
will could be seen as variations on his viewpoint. For
Aquinas, free will is the power by which a man is able to
judge freely. Judgement belongs to reason, but freedom
of judgement belongs to the will. Aquinas does not refer
to any kind of judgement, but to the decisive judgement
of choice which puts an end to the deliberation which
arises from the fact that a person can consider a possible
object of choice from different points of view. Thus the
'decisive judgement' is made under the influence of the
will.

For Hume (1740, p. 399), the will is 'nothing but the
internal impression we feel and are conscious of, when
we knowingly give rise to any new motion of our body,
or new perception of our mind'. For Kant (1785), the will
and practical reason, or reason in its practical, moral use
or function, are interconnected. Practical reason both
influences the will and can be identified with it, so that
the will is a rational power and not a blind drive. For
Kant there is no theoretical proof that a rational being is
free, but the moral law compels us to assume it. Practical
reason or the will of a rational being must regard itself as
free; that is, the will of such a being cannot have a will of
its own, or be autonomous, without the idea of freedom.
The idea of freedom is, for Kant, practically necessary, a
necessary condition for making autonomous and moral
choices.

Few thinkers, past or present, seem to have taken full
account of the existence of the unconscious, or have
dismissed its role as of no account in these matters. Man

is still seen as predominantly rational. Reason is either
theoretical or practical reason, but never unconscious
reason, which is the psychoanalytic currency. Hume,
however, cautioned against any simplistic division of man
into reason and will, and also considered that reason
alone could never be a motive for any action of the will.
Indeed he argued that 'reason is and ought to be the slave
of the passions, and can never pretend to any other office
than to serve and obey them' (1740, p. 415).

Although it seems difficult to find answers to the questions
posed above, I think that some of them are central to
psychoanalysis in quite an ordinary way. Many analysands come to the analyst complaining of a feeling of
estrangement from themselves, or of being passive by-
standers to forces beyond their power, or of being in
great conflict about what to do. They may have an incapacity to make decisive judgements, or else repeatedly
decide what is not in their or other people's interests, as
in suicidal cases. That is, they complain of not having a
will of their own, or of being weak-willed and confused,
constantly doing what they think they ought not to be
doing. It is usually taken for granted that these are
acceptable reasons for analysis, and that analysis should
be able to 'free' the analysand to get on with his life.

By and large the analyst probably does not think much
about the questions I have raised while he is seeing the
analysand, the treatment being too engaging for that. Nor
can the analyst wait for a satisfactory and coherent answer
to questions of this kind, for he must get on with the task
in hand. That is, the analyst cannot rely on hard evidence
for these and many other questions, as he is constantly
moving beyond having to wait for all the evidence in
order to make interpretations and create useful conjec-
tures. And in a sense, evidence arises hand in hand
with interpretation. As William James put it (quoted in
Passmore, p. 101), there are many questions on which we
are bound to make up our minds, whether we like it or
not, although the evidence is far from satisfactory. Such

evidence as there is comes from consistent observations and hypothesis formation, as a result of the analyst's objective attitude; as well as the use of the less definable and more 'loose' aspect of the analyst's own human attitude, which John Klauber, throughout his work, highlighted.

The analyst is engaged in a relationship in which there is a subtle mixture of the objective attitude and the ordinary human attitude appropriate to ordinary human relations. In analysis there is a certain amount of suspension of ordinary human relationships in the service of the treatment, but not too much, especially as the problem for the analysand has so often been precisely that of the suspension or breakdown of such relations. To understand free will and psychoanalysis, then, it is important to look at some of the acknowledged and unacknowledged assumptions of psychoanalysis, which one could divide into assumptions specific to psychoanalysis, and assumptions common to other disciplines.

1. There are so many different analytic assumptions that it is difficult to be certain of making any commonly acceptable statement, and opinions differ widely on theory and practice. This could be interpreted as evidence of psychoanalytic chaos, but it may also indicate a rich variety of approaches. One could say that most, if not all, psychoanalysts assume three basic postulates: first, the existence and importance of the unconscious and psychic conflict between the unconscious and consciousness; second, the existence of sexuality in psychic life; and third, the need to look at the transference in analytic treatment. One could see the unconscious and the transference as the most 'determined' and 'universal' elements of the triad. That is, psychoanalysis has discovered that the unconscious has its own laws, which are not those of conscious reason, and yet none the less involve causal assumptions. Psychoanalysis has also discovered the repeated and spontaneous occurrence of the transference in all analytic treatment, which again can be seen as evidence of a causal psychic network. Sexuality, however,

refers to a more ill-defined and vague area of knowledge
and functioning; sexual concepts are much looser than
other analytic concepts and have almost undefined limits,
evidence perhaps of a 'freer' or less determined network
of thinking.

2. Psychoanalysts often use, consciously or unconsciously, assumptions which are common to literature
and philosophy. One particular and central assumption
is that detailed observation and enquiry of a situation will
lead to understanding a person's motives, and that there
is a constancy in human nature that makes it susceptible
to understanding. In Hume's words, 'The most irregular
and unexpected resolutions of men may frequently be
accounted for by those who know every particular cir-
cumstance of character or situation' (1751, p. 88). This
statement is parallel to Freud's notion of the need for a
complete psychoanalytic reconstruction of the subject's
history, in order fully to understand his symptoms and
behaviour.

I also think that analysts, consciously or unconsciously,
tend to use at least two different models of freedom of
the will. Either they see every communication by the
analysand as being determined, which is the model of
strict determinism; or they tend to keep in mind some-
where the notion of an area that cannot and should not
be determined, and so follow a model which acknowl-
edges the area of absolute freedom of the will, or at least
an area of spontaneity. A strict interpretation of the
doctrine of freedom would imply that no human actions
can be predicted or even understood, and a strict interpretation of the doctrine of determinism would imply that all
actions can be predicted and understood. Obviously for
most practical purposes, and certainly in the analytic
setting, one is using a mixture of the two. Necessity and
free will are not arch rivals in analysis but rather two
poles of a continuum.

Thus, in attempting to formulate the relationship between psychoanalysis and the problem of freedom of the
will, there would also seem to be two 'poles' – on the

one hand, the attitude of a fairly strict determinism, with an attempt to fit the analysand with psychoanalytic knowledge tightly, like a tight-fitting suit; and on the other hand, the ambiguous and ill-defined sense of the analysand's freedom to act and think. These differences are reflected in the philosophical literature on the topic of freedom of the will, which is immense and often confusing. Some authors come down firmly on the side of strict determinism, others on the side of absolute freedom of the will; while others, with whom I am personally sympathetic, attempt to steer a difficult middle course, known as 'compatibilism'. They accept a certain amount of determinism as necessary and compatible with a certain amount of freedom of the will. For example, Ayer argues that the very use of the word 'determinism' is misleading.

For it tends to suggest that one event is somehow in the power of another, whereas the truth is merely that they are factually correlated. When an event of one type occurs, an event of another type occurs also, in a certain temporal or spatio-temporal relation to the first. The rest is only metaphor. And it is because of the metaphor, and not because of the fact, that we come to think that there is an antithesis between causality and freedom. (1954, p. 22)

None the less, in spite of Ayer's statement, it does not seem easy to define the appropriate boundaries for those who feel the middle course is both philosophically and psychoanalytically appropriate. In order to attempt some clarification of the situation, it might help to state some basic freedoms that are often assumed, rightly or wrongly, in the understanding of an analysis. It may be obvious, and yet it is still important to establish the basic freedoms that we assume or prevent.

First of all, psychoanalysis is a voluntary undertaking. And yet even this statement is far from being simple. After all, until an analysand has begun an analysis, he or she does not know what they are in for, and by the time that

they do it may be too late for them to opt out freely.
Indeed, the early part of an analysis perhaps requires a particularly sensitive handling of this whole dilemma until the analysand is convinced that he or she has a choice about coming to sessions, if indeed it is considered that such a choice is both possible and desirable.

I myself would suggest, following Freud (1913), that the analyst's attitude in the early stages of the analysis should be different from that of other stages. In particular, it is important to foster the development of a process of enquiry by not making interpretations too soon, or by 'fitting' the analysand with the 'analytic suit' too quickly. A finely balanced teasing out of themes and letting the imagos 'have their say' may be more important than the use of the 'high power' of the analytic microscope at this time.

Whatever the rights and wrongs of the 'opening' technique, there still remains the delicate area of the question of how much the analysis is undertaken freely. And apart from this area, one could argue that there are certain liberties that the analysand has the right to expect: e.g., liberty of opinion, expression and personal possessions; and no arbitrary invasion of such basic rights. That is, though the analysand gives up a certain amount of freedom (often a considerable amount) to the analyst, this should not be so much that such basic liberties are interfered with. That is, the analysand has the right to an area of freedom which entails that he is not degraded. This would be consistent with an absence of coercion, freedom from undue interference with personal liberty (see Mill's essay 'On liberty', 1859), and the preservation of his human essence.

Yet there are a number of physical and psychic restraints which do hinder the analysand's freedom. There is, for example, an absence of physical freedom – one of the most basic freedoms – owing to the fact that the analysand's body is confined by being on the couch. As Schopenhauer put it in his essay on freedom of the will, 'Most frequently we conceive of freedom as an attribute of animate things, whose distinctive feature is the ability to originate movements from their own free will, that is voluntarily. Thus such movements are called free when no material obstacles prevent them' (1841, p. 3). Schopenhauer described this physical meaning of the concept of freedom as the original, immediate and most frequent one, but considered that 'moral freedom', which includes consideration of the role of self-consciousness, is the higher form of freedom, involved in the problem of freedom of the will.

I would suggest, too, that in the analytic situation physical freedom is curtailed in the service of *another* freedom. To clarify the meaning of this new freedom, I have turned to the philosopher Harry Frankfurt and his essay 'Freedom of the will and the concept of a person' (1971). In Frankfurt's view, the essential difference between 'persons' and other creatures is to be found in the structure of a person's will. Humans and animals have desires and motives and make choices. But what is peculiarly human is the capacity to form what he calls 'second order' desires and volitions.

Besides wanting and choosing, and being moved to do this or that, men may also want to have (or not to have) certain desires and motives. They are capable of wanting to be different, in their preferences and purposes, from what they are ... Someone has a desire of the second order either when he wants simply to have a certain desire or when he wants a certain desire to be his will ... having the freedom to do what he wants is not a sufficient condition of having a free will ... A person's will is only free if he is free to have the will he wants. (1971, pp. 82–3)

In this viewpoint, the kind of freedom that is specifically human, and which I think is central to psychoanalysis, is not merely the capacity to do what one wants, but to be free to want what one wants. I would thus suggest that psychoanalysis is primarily concerned with second-order desires and volitions, many of which are essentially unconscious. In particular, psychoanalysis starts with the premise that freedom of the will is a problem, and that a 'person' is the entity for whom this is a special problem.

An alternative way of putting the proposition would be to consider freedom as a special kind of determinism, one involved in choosing a path. This has been vividly portrayed in poetic form in the beginning of the *Inferno*, where Dante finds himself in a dark wood in which he has completely lost the path. With his father-like guide Virgil (not unlike an analyst), Dante finally discovers which path is his, but only after a journey through the depths of inferno and purgatory. As in the case of the analyst and the analysand, Virgil does not accompany Dante into paradise but only shows him the way, which he is free to follow or not. Some people can only choose one path, others can never choose any path. Freedom could be understood to be the ability to choose one or more paths, or at the very least to determine the mode of travel.

There is a danger in analysis, however, that the analyst will be tempted to join the analysand at the end of the journey and not disengage, and then the whole process will have been in vain. The other temptation is to push the analysand in directions chosen by the analyst.

The ethic of Christianity teaches that the end of human conduct is to be found in God, that happiness can be found in the love of God (as with Dante in paradise), i.e., that the object of happiness can be obtained. The ethic of psychoanalysis is both more anxiety-provoking and frustrating, and yet more respectful of the subject's freedom of will, for in the analytic situation (unlike the real world of social relationships) the object of love, i.e., the analyst, can never be obtained as such. The analysand has to keep searching for his second-order desires and volitions because of the very nature of the psychoanalytic situation of frustration, or 'tease' (see Klauber, 1981, p. 39).

At first sight, the psychoanalytic situation would seem to involve considerable restraint on the part of the analyst, and considerable letting go on the part of the analysand, who is supposed to offer his associations without censorship. While the analysand's freedom to act is limited but put in the service of free association, the analyst's freedom to act and to reveal himself is also limited, but is at the service of knowledge of the analysand's desires and volitions. Thus, while the analyst's freedom is limited, so is his bondage. Indeed, the analyst's capacity to free associate to himself in the session may be an important monitor of a creative attitude, and of a creative 'spark' being possible in the space between analyst and analysand. I think that this highlights the fact that in the analytic setting, a monitor of the analysand's freedom, or capacity to be free, is the degree to which he allows freedom to the other/analyst.

There is a further complication concerning the question of the freedom of the will peculiar to psychoanalysis, and the source of a subtle change in the way that one may conceive the nature of the problem. For the most part, the question of freedom of the will is raised in relation to conscious knowledge or traditional reason; for example, a decisive judgement is a conscious activity, however much it is imbued with faith and belief. Yet with psychoanalysis, there is an unconscious knowledge which is far more determining and decisive for the human subject. One may then ask how the subject can be free with respect to a knowledge of which he is not, and may never be, totally conscious, and of which he can only obtain glimpses, e.g., in dreams, jokes, and fragments of waking life, or in the especially favoured analytic setting. One may also ask if the existence of this unconscious knowledge significantly changes the nature of our conception of freedom of the will.

The answer to these questions would certainly involve a strange kind of freedom, one which requires a subtle interplay between the known and the unknown. It would certainly appear that the notions of freedom and of knowledge are intimately linked. For example, one can argue, as Stuart Hampshire does in *Freedom of the*

Individual, that the more the subject knows the less likelihood there is that he is going to act in a manner which does not in fact lie within his power. That is – up to a point – the more one knows of oneself the more free one is, or rather the more choices there are available, although (taken too literally) this may lead to confusion or to an over-intellectual attitude to ordinary life.

I think that it is possible that freedom of the will is a useful concept of psychoanalysis, whatever its philosophical status, because not to use it (or some similar concept) may be dangerous and cramping for the psychoanalytic treatment. I would also tend to think that there is, in the psychoanalytic treatment setting, a private area in both analyst and analysand which is often being touched, consciously or unconsciously. It is an area, to use Winnicott's ideas (1971a), involved with creativity and play. It is a spontaneous area from which arise new links and connections, and which can be conceptualized using the notion of freedom of the will. It is perhaps the most 'real' part of the analyst and analysand. It may also be linked to the probability that the psyche is rather a loose and open-ended collection of functions and not a unified total entity.

I grant that it is quite possible that the existence of such an area is a mere illusion, however necessary such an illusion may be. One may recall in this context the words of Spinoza.

Further conceive that a stone, while continuing in motion, should be capable of thinking and knowing, that it is endeavouring, as far as it can, to continue to move. Such a stone, being conscious merely of its own endeavour and not at all indifferent, would believe itself to be completely free, and would think that it continued in motion solely because of its own wish. This is that human freedom, which all boast that they possess, and which consists solely in the fact that men are conscious of their own desires, but are ignorant of the causes whereby that

78 *desire has been determined.* (1678, vol. 2, Letter LXII, pp. 390–1)

Thus the ordinary notion of freedom is for Spinoza mere illusion, due to ignorance of the true causes. For him genuine freedom is knowledge of causes; and the life of the free man is the one free of external causes, because of this knowledge.

I am certain that I have not fully answered the questions I posed at the beginning of the paper, but I hope that I have at least raised some further questions, and I would like to summarize my thinking at this point. The analysand does have a special kind of freedom in an analysis, although his freedom is controlled in certain ways; the analysand's choice about what is happening to him is a delicate one, especially at the beginning of treatment; the analyst can facilitate, or interfere with, the analysand's freedom, and second-order volitions and desires are the 'special currency' of analysis. I have outlined some of the acceptable limits to the analysand's freedom in terms of basic liberties; I have suggested some aspects of what may or may not be determined in analysis, and I have suggested that the concept of freedom of the will is essential to analysis – and is anyway incorporated, consciously or unconsciously, into much of what is practised. Finally I have suggested that psychoanalysis has discovered a conception of freedom of the will which incorporates the existence of unconscious knowledge.

Patrick Casement

I WISH to discuss here the re-experiencing of trauma in the transference and some aspects of its treatment in analysis. I also wish to consider ways in which, sometimes, the analytic relationship itself can become traumatic to a patient.

SOME TERMS DEFINED

IN *The Language of Psycho-Analysis*, Laplanche and Pontalis describe *psychical trauma* as: 'An event in the subject's life defined by its intensity, by the subject's incapacity to respond adequately to it, and by the upheaval and long-lasting effects that it brings about in the psychical organization' (1973, p. 465). However, not every experience of trauma is, at a specific moment, traumatic (Khan, 1963). *Silent trauma* (Hoffer, 1952) is used here to refer to the effects of cumulative stress, whether in childhood or in the course of analytic therapy. This is often difficult to deal with because the causes are less clear than with more specific trauma.

In this chapter I wish to emphasize the double nature of *transference*. To quote from Klauber (this volume, p. 7): 'The transference illusion is not simply a false perception or a false belief, but the manifestation of the similarity of the subjective experience aroused by an event in the past and in the present.' I think of this area of illusion as the *overlap between past and present* (Casement, 1985, pp. 6–8).

The patient's experience of the analytic relationship is not entirely an illusion; and it is certainly not all transference. There are often elements of objective reality that function as triggers for transference (Gill, 1982; Langs, 1978). This is part of what I understand Klauber to be referring to when he speaks of the need for 'horizontal analysis' (of what is happening in the here and now), alongside 'vertical analysis' (the historical approach to transference). In the unpublished fifth University College lecture he says of this horizontal dimension in the analytic relationship: 'What had been experienced in the past was also being enacted in a relationship between two people in the present.' This enactment, in some measure, involves the analyst as well as the patient.

In defining *anxiety as a signal*, Laplanche and Pontalis write: 'The signal of anxiety is a reproduction in attenuated form of the anxiety reaction originally experienced in a traumatic situation: it makes it possible for defensive operations to be set in motion' (1973, p. 422).

Finally, following Matte Blanco (1975), I believe it is helpful (particularly when considering the re-experiencing of trauma) to think in terms of *unconscious sets*. This enables us to recognize why the mind unconsciously registers particular elements of traumatic experience as belonging together – because once they were specifically experienced together. They have thus come to be established as linked, timelessly and without exception. The result is that any of these associated elements can come to represent the whole experience, of which the trauma had been a part, and may therefore trigger signal anxiety as if that trauma were about to be repeated. And if several

of these associated elements happen to occur together,
there is a heightened sense of trauma again being about
to happen.

In order to embody these definitions, I shall give two
clinical vignettes. In the first example, we can see signal
anxiety occurring in response to a set of associations that
may still have been conscious.

UNCONSCIOUS SETS IN THE MAKING

Example 1

A BABY GIRL of one year was taken by her mother for
inoculation, prior to going abroad. Before injecting the
baby's thigh, the doctor asked her mother to pull up the
baby's dress. Up to this point nothing unfamiliar was
happening, except (perhaps) for the presence of this
comparative stranger – the family doctor. However, after
being shocked by the sudden pain of the injection, it was
some months before this child was able to recover from
the experience. It seemed to be forever imminent. Most
specifically, she demonstrated clear signal anxiety whenever her mother tried to change her clothes.

Any attempts by the mother to pull up the child's dress
were reacted to by screaming. A similar response was
evident upon removing other garments; the nearer to the
lower half of her body the more intense was the reaction.
Other people were trusted with more undressing of the
child than the mother, but nobody was allowed to pull
up her dress.

We can see in this example how various associations
relating to the danger situation had been established
around the original trauma. The most specific were the
following: *the mother holding her baby on her lap* and
pulling up the dress. Lesser associations could be identified too: *clothes near to the thigh*, and *people like the
mother*. It was noticeable that the father was trusted more
than the mother, when the child was on his lap instead of
hers. But when the child was on someone else's lap, the

82 father became a source of anxiety if he then held out hands to help with any undressing.

Therefore, it would seem, there were different levels of association operating: a lap-person who was a woman being feared more than a lap-person who was a man, particularly if associated with trying to remove clothing. Also, a man holding out hands to help, if associated with trying to remove clothing, was feared more than a woman holding out hands to help.

In this example we can see that the trauma came to be associated with a set of principal elements: *being on a woman's lap: clothes being removed or lifted; a man holding out hands to do something.*

The mother, intuitively recognizing the associations to which her child was responding, found a way of dealing with this problem. She created differences by putting the child into a bath rather than try to undress her on her lap. She was then able to remove clothes that were wet rather than dry. Wet clothes had not been any part of the original trauma, so this difference enabled the child to accept a new way of being undressed even though *removing clothes* was still part of what the mother was doing. She was, therefore, not completely avoiding the feared experience but finding a way of facing it – as much of it as the child was yet able to tolerate. Gradually, the associative links became weaker and dry clothes could be removed too: first, if removed while sitting in an empty bath, and (eventually) while sitting on mother's lap.

UNCONSCIOUS SETS IN THE TRANSFERENCE

IN THE SECOND EXAMPLE we can see evidence of signal anxiety in response to a set of associations that was more clearly unconscious.

Example 2

A MALE PATIENT aged twenty-five sometimes experienced acute anxiety between sessions and over weekends.

He sometimes had the phantasy that I had become ill or had died. If the telephone rang at such a time as this, he became afraid to answer it – as if this were bringing confirmation of his phantasy. What then was happening in the transference? It emerged in the analysis that in his early teens the patient had begun to face his father with difficult feelings he had never previously shown so directly to him. In the course of these confrontations he had begun to communicate much that had earlier seemed entirely taboo. For example, he had expressed extreme resentment at the emotional distance that had existed between them for all the remembered years prior to this, and anger at his father for preferring his younger sister.

In the course of several weeks there were crucial changes taking place in this father–son relationship. Most particularly, the son was *expressing difficult feelings* and he was *being listened to*. Previously he had imagined that he could never dare to confront his father in this way: 'It would have killed him.'

The son was now discovering, to his surprise, that it was actually safe to be this direct with his father. What was more, he discovered that he could also love his father as well as hate him. Then, one day when the patient was at school, the news was *telephoned* through to say that his father had suffered a pulmonary embolism and had died.

What had been happening in the transference could be better understood once we had identified some of the unconscious links to a past set of experiences. There were several similarities between the time before the father's death and what was happening in the patient's analysis: he was talking with a man whom he sometimes experienced as his father; in the transference he was confronting the analyst with his anger and his criticism; he was being listened to. These experiences were then followed by an absence – the analyst not being there. Because there had been a similar set of experiences associated with the father's death, absence at a critical time had come to be unconsciously equated with death. The telephone was therefore being feared as the means by which news of this death would reach the patient.

In the transference illusion, I had become (between sessions) the dead father. The patient's distress at his father's death, being re-experienced in these ways, could then be brought to sessions where I (who had not died) could help the patient with his feelings about my 'death' (his father's death) during these times of absence. His mother, too distressed herself at the time, had not been able to help him in this way. For years, therefore, the patient had felt that only his father would have been able to understand how impossible his death had been for the patient to bear. But his father, being dead, could not be there to help him. So, it seemed as if no one would ever be able to understand, or to help him with, the effects of his father's death upon him – and the timing of it.

DOUBLENESS IN THE TRANSFERENCE

WE CAN SEE HERE a theme which runs throughout this chapter – that of the double nature of the transference. Clinical findings show that a patient needs to discover enough that is different in the analytic relationship to represent security, for it then to be possible for the patient to tolerate the re-experiencing of trauma in the transference. Elements of similarity in the analytic situation are then used to represent traumatic experience as it was. Both dimensions are necessary, the similarity as well as the difference, for the analytic experience to be therapeutic.

Therefore, if the analyst is obtrusively different (from whichever key person in the patient's life), the patient feels deflected from using the analyst in the transference to represent that particular object of intense or difficult feelings. But, if there is too much similarity, the analytic experience threatens to be too nearly a repetition of earlier experiences, which could preclude recognizing this as transference. The analysis may then break down, the patient either leaving treatment for safety – or seeking refuge in renewed defences against this further trauma now being re-enacted in the analysis. *Sufficient similarity* is necessary to sustain the transference illusion, but *sufficient difference* is also necessary if this is not to become traumatic in itself.

I shall now give examples of both kinds of failure in analytic working with the patient; too much similarity, and the masquerade of too much difference.

Example 3

A THERAPIST in supervision with me confessed to feeling irritable with a patient who kept on complaining about her mother: she felt very identified with the mother of this complaining child. In her countertransference response to this patient she was becoming alienated from her patient's experience, due to a failure in empathy. The patient, therefore, could not get beyond feeling stuck in her therapy with a therapist who was being perceived as 'just like' her irritable mother (Sandler, 1976). The problem relationship being complained of was thus being brought directly into the therapy: it was not merely being talked about. However, until this was understood, the patient's transference experience had remained all too real to be analysed. The patient was once again in the presence of a mother-person who was failing to recognize the extent to which she had been shutting off from the patient's feelings. The traumatic degree of similarity between the therapist and the mother had continued to block this therapy.

The patient may, however, have been prompting her therapist (as with her mother) to recognize that she had a resistance to being truly in touch with what the patient was feeling. Therefore, the therapist had to restore a sense of difference between herself as therapist and herself as the transference-mother before the patient's experience of the transference could be analysed. Antipathy had to give way to empathy. With this recovery the therapy could proceed more freely.

In the next example the therapist (at least manifestly) had seemed to be different from the patient's parents.

Example 4

A MALE PATIENT came into analysis because he had come to realize that there was something he had never been able to deal with during his previous therapy: he still had difficulty with anger – his own and other people's. In his analysis it appeared that this patient's previous therapist had always been too nice to him for it to be possible to be angry with her. He reported the following interchange, which took place when he discussed the possibility of his going back into therapy with her. The patient had said: 'I could never be *angry* with you.' To this the therapist had apparently replied: 'Was there really so much to be angry about?' The patient now realized that his anger had regularly been deflected during that therapy, the therapist thus preventing him from using her analytically in any negative transference. The patient felt that his anger had been treated as unjustified – much as it had been by his parents. It had not been accepted as belonging to the transference.

In the subsequent analysis, anger could only be analysed when the analyst was found to be able to tolerate being used by the patient to represent the mother or father, towards whom he still felt angry, with the analyst surviving the experience of being battered with much that had remained unresolved from the patient's childhood. It was crucial that he could cope with direct expressions of anger.

In this patient's analysis there was evidence to suggest that the previous therapist had been attempting to be a better parent, in trying to be someone who deserved gratitude rather than anger. Because of this, the therapist had unwittingly become traumatically like the patient's actual parents, who had likewise behaved as if there could be no valid occasion for this child to be angry with them.

Analysis of the negative transference had therefore not
been possible.

From the conscious viewpoint of the therapist, these two examples may seem to be quite different. But when viewed from the perspective of a patient's unconscious perception, they are actually very similar. The therapist in Example 3 had become too much like the patient's mother; but she was consciously aware of being discomforted by the irritation that her patient was regularly evoking in her, and she was seeking help in supervision with this difficulty. The therapist in Example 4 seems to have made efforts to be actively different from the patient's parents. The patient was consciously grateful to her until he recognized that there were unresolved problems with anger (perhaps in his therapist as well as in himself).

The point that I am trying to illustrate here is that any attempt at 'being the better parent' has the effect of deflecting, even seducing, a patient from using the analyst or therapist in a negative transference (see Langs, 1978).

THE 'AS IF' RELATIONSHIP

THESE TWO EXAMPLES illustrate how important it is to preserve the 'as if' quality of the analytic relationship. It is this illusion that allows a patient to re-experience in the transference whatever aspects of earlier relationships are being brought into the analysis, *as if* the analyst really were the original person to whom the patient is currently feeling related. Therefore, when trauma is being brought into the transference, it is the illusion of realness that accounts for the transference experience being so immediate. But, if this is not to become traumatic too, there needs to be an adequate sense of safety in the analytic 'holding' for it to be tolerable for the patient also to re-experience extremes of unsafety in the transference. Only thus can a patient find a viable security amidst the transference illusion of trauma re-experienced, without which there will not be room for the patient to 'play' with that experience. And without play, as Winnicott points out, there can be no psychotherapy (1971a, p. 54).

Of course, if a traumatic similarity is too pronounced, whether manifest or latent, there may be no analytic space within which to analyse this as transference. From the patient's viewpoint it is then no longer experienced as transference but as real repetition. This cannot be analysed. It must first be remedied (if it can be) so that the potential space (Winnicott, 1971a, pp. 100–110) of the analytic relationship is re-established. Only thus can a patient 'create' such transference as can at that moment be tolerated.

If, however, a therapist insists on being experienced as different from the original object or objects (as in the last example) there can be no analysable transference in that area of relating. At best there can only be 'charismatic cure', which evokes change by seduction. And, when this difference is based upon defensive behaviour by the therapist, the repetition becomes more insidious – because it is concealed. It may then continue to be beyond the conscious awareness of either party, and so remain not dealt with.

SILENT TRAUMA

W H A T   W E   C A N also learn from the examples just given is that there are times when the analytic experience itself develops into trauma. This can happen when the patient senses something wrong in the analytic relationship that is not being dealt with, as in Example 3 – where the therapist had been switched off because of feeling irritable; or when there is something more radically wrong that cannot readily be dealt with, as in Example 4 – where the therapist seemed to have unresolved problems that were parallel to those of the patient. In each of these cases, while the therapist's own behaviour remained unattended to, the analytic process was being deflected or hindered. Patients do not always regard this kind of failure as traumatic, but the effects upon the analytic work can be long-lasting. To this extent, therefore, I regard this as silent trauma, fitting the definition of trauma with which we started.

There are other cases where the patient becomes more obviously traumatized by the experience of therapy or analysis, but for reasons that are often not at all clear. In these cases, the childhood may not have been clearly traumatic, except perhaps cumulatively over a long period of time (Khan, 1963). The behaviour of the analyst, likewise, may not be significantly traumatic in any of the ways so far described; and yet the patient becomes unable to work in the analysis.

I believe that this hold-up in an analysis can sometimes be provoked by aspects of the analytic setting, or by the analyst's way of working. It therefore needs to be noted that, if a particular style of analysis is rigidly adhered to, because this is considered to be classical technique and therefore 'correct', it may take much longer for the analyst to recognize when problems in an analysis may actually arise from a patient's response to the analyst's way of working.*

Analysts, therefore, have to be careful that they do not hold too strongly to their own clinical style. Some character defences (in the analyst) may be rationalized as technique; then the patient has problems which the analyst may see as unrelated to himself. For example, a patient's behaviour may be due to desperation about a

* Since writing this, my attention has been drawn to Ferenczi's comments on the same issue. Symington (1986, p. 197) writes:

... Ferenczi stressed that the distant attitude in sessions was not helpful to the patient because it so often re-enacted a past trauma. In 'The principles of relaxation and neocatharsis' he [Ferenczi] says: 'We find that the rigid and cool aloofness on the analyst's part was experienced by the patient as a continuation of his infantile struggle with the grown-ups' authority, and made him repeat the same reactions in character and symptoms as formed the basis of the real neurosis' (1930, pp. 117–8).

communication failure in the analysis, but it can be mistaken for resistance. Analysts sometimes become defensive too! It then becomes much harder for the patient to offer corrective cues (Casement, 1985; Langs, 1978). That is why it is important to have a technique that allows room for unconscious prompting by the patient – as this makes it easier for analysts to become aware of their own defensiveness or their countertransference. The possibility of movement in the analysis can then be restored.

I wish now to give two examples where patients were temporarily stuck in their analyses with me. In each case the problem turned out to be due to traumatic similarities between my way of working and the way that each patient had experienced a parent. Renewed progress only became possible when the reasons for stalemate had been recognized and dealt with. This required a flexibility in technique.

Example 5

THIS CLINICAL SEQUENCE is from work with a patient early in my analytic career. Mrs G, as I shall call her, often used to complain about her parents, who had become separated and divorced by the time she was seven: she was an only child. She described her mother as someone who was distant and unresponsive, who thought she always knew best, and who frequently saw faults in others but never in herself. Her mother could not tolerate criticism, and if Mrs G ever made perceptive comments about her she would be accused of being out of her mind: 'You must be crazy even to think such things of your own mother' would be a typical response. Her father was mostly absent from her life.

In her analysis Mrs G became very stuck. She would often lie silent and paralysed. Interpretations, even if accepted, did not help. Instead, she came to feel persecuted by any attempt of mine to interpret; she experienced this as my trying to 'see into her.' She once remarked: 'My mother used to say that she could tell what I was thinking, and it often felt as if she did.'

The patient increasingly came to see the analytic relationship as traumatically similar to her experience of her parents. For instance, her mother (like a caricature analyst) used not to answer personal questions; instead, she would often parry with other questions, or she would query the patient's motives in asking such questions of her. The father, by contrast, remained a shadowy presence in the background. Mrs G thus came to see me as just like these parents. This was very difficult to treat simply as transference, as these parents had (in some respects) behaved much as I then used to think analytic technique required me to behave.

For this patient, therefore, the analytic setting and the usual techniques of analysis had *in themselves* become a traumatic repetition of her childhood relationships. As a result she became unable to recognize the transference dimension within this context of sameness. She had to discover a sufficient difference between me and her parents before she could resume working analytically with me.

I shall not describe in any detail the prolonged period of analysis during which this problem was being worked out. In essence, I had to discover ways of being more flexible with the patient. For instance, when Mrs G asked me a personal question she used to defend herself from a rebuff by saying: 'Of course, I know you won't answer that.' Sometimes, to her surprise, I chose to give her a straight answer. Also, when she had accurately read what I was thinking or feeling, I would sometimes affirm her impression rather than fend it off.

In ways like these Mrs G was able to elicit responses from me that she had not been able to get from her parents, and which she likewise did not expect from an analyst. Naturally, I had to watch carefully for repercussions from such self-revelations, but the gains in the analysis clearly outweighed the occasional difficulties that arose from this openness.

Mrs G eventually became able to discover for herself the paradox of transference, becoming able to explore the recurring sense of sameness within a growing awareness of difference in the analytic relationship. Gradually she recovered from the paralysing conviction that I was really just the same as her parents. She could then more freely use me in the transference *to represent* the relationship difficulties that she had had with each of her parents, which continued to be the paramount focus of the analytic work. This had not been deflected by the evidence of difference: it was this, in the end, that had made it possible to analyse the patient's transference experience.

In the following clinical sequence, I can illustrate something more of this discovery of difference – beyond a traumatic sense of similarity.

Example 6

AS AN INFANT, Mr H had often been left to choke upon his own crying. He used then to experience his mother as having abandoned him. A phantasy was subsequently developed whereby this abandonment had been seen as related to the intensity of his need for his mother's attention. The more intensely he needed this the more sure he became that he would be abandoned. Silences in the analysis were frequently experienced as abandonment or as retaliation. This did not mean that I therefore felt this patient should be protected from all silences; but it was clear I should monitor the degree of anxiety that he could tolerate – and space my silences accordingly.

A technical problem here was that Mr H also expected me to be unable to tolerate the intensity of his anxiety and his anger. Therefore, if I responded too quickly to a silence I was seen as afraid of his violent reaction to my silences. Gradually, I came to realize that the transference experience sometimes became so total for Mr H that the therapeutic alliance was in jeopardy or seemed to be entirely absent.

Eventually Mr H pointed me towards a way of beginning to deal with this problem. He began to complain that the lights in my room made his eyes ache. Would I please turn off the light in front of him during his sessions? I then recalled a discussion, with Dr Martin James, of his paper 'Premature ego development' (1960). In this discussion, Dr James had made the following statement: 'All analysis has to be conducted within the omnipotence of the patient, which has to be challenged sensitively and very very cautiously.' He later illustrated this by giving an example of a patient who needed him 'to provide the basic sameness of the initial mothering, within the analytic situation, before the patient could tolerate change and thus begin to grow'.

The impression I had of my patient's mother was that she had become prematurely unavailable to him. I, therefore, did not think there had been an adequate preparation for this sudden distance. There had been no 'progressive failure to adapt' (Winnicott, 1965, pp. 87 ff.). Maybe, then, Mr H needed me to provide symbolic evidence of my basic sameness, as a thread of continuity by which he could hold on to me (as someone still controlled by him), while he was experiencing intensely violent feelings towards me – as towards the mother who had remained unresponsive to him even when he had been most needy.

For about six months I regularly turned off the offending light. In doing this I was responding to what I regarded as a need that should be met. I was not simply trying to placate the patient; rather, my flexibility here signified a difference from his parents that freed him sufficiently to rage at me in the transference – for instance over my silences or my failures to understand. Inevitably, I sometimes forgot to turn off the light. I had then to pay for that too, and in no uncertain terms – the patient using that tangible failure to rage at me, as against failures in the early holding environment, in ways so well described by Winnicott (Winnicott, 1958, p. 281; 1965, p. 258).

As we worked through what was required in this phase of the analysis, Mr H became able to relinquish his token of control. When he was ready, *he* told *me* one day that he could cope with the light being left on. This meant he could begin to use me as someone able to survive his rages. Now that my separateness from him was being more clearly established, he was more able to explore his murderous attacks upon me in dreams and in his waking thoughts.

THE CORRECTIVE EMOTIONAL EXPERIENCE

I WISH TO CONCLUDE by considering the concept of *the corrective emotional experience*, originally proposed by Alexander (1954), and more recently resurrected by Elizabeth Moberly in her book *The Psychology of Self and Other* (Moberly, 1985).

It is a seductive idea that what our patients might be needing, for recovery from past bad experience, is an analyst willing to provide opportunities for good experiences as a substitute for those that had been lacking in childhood. But things are not so easily changed in the internal world of the patient.

The analytic 'good object' is not someone better than the original object: it is someone who survives being treated as a 'bad object'. By surviving I mean neither collapsing under that experience nor retaliating because of it (Winnicott, 1971a, p. 91).

Example 7

IN MY CHAPTER 'Analytic holding under pressure' (Casement, 1985, pp. 155–67), I describe a patient, Mrs B, who reached a point where she felt she could not possibly go on with her analysis unless I would let her hold my hand if the reliving of an early trauma became too unbearable. I will not go over the clinical sequence in full here; but, as the case illustrates my present argument most clearly, I shall draw out a few of its significant features and discuss it in a slightly different way.

At the age of eleven months Mrs B had been badly burned, and six months later her scars were operated on under a local anaesthetic. In the course of her analysis, she began to experience me as the surgeon who had operated on her, and became utterly terrified of me. During that operation her mother, who was holding her hands, had fainted. In telling me that she might need to hold my hand, she was appealing to me to be available to her as a mother who would protect her from the transference experience of me as the surgeon.

Under pressure, and aware of the extremity of her early experience, I agreed that she might need this possibility. However, over the ensuing weekend I gave much thought to the implications for Mrs B if I offered myself as a 'better mother', and I realized that this could be a collusion with her wish to avoid the worst part of her experience by not facing it *as it was*.

In her next session the patient brought a dream and its waking continuation which showed that she too was aware of the implications of my offer, for she saw me as about to become a collapsed analyst. Following this unconscious prompt from the patient, I withdrew the possibility of holding my hand. Gradually, and after much difficulty, Mrs B came to recognize that I was prepared to remain analyst rather than collapse when in touch with the intensity of what she was feeling.

The patient's subsequent use of me in the transference came to include the experience of not being physically held – after her mother had fainted. I then had to be able to face the impact of the patient's feelings from that time. And, eventually, Mrs B could find that I had survived in my own right; not by some manipulation of the clinical situation, nor by her continuing to protect me from what she experienced as the worst within herself (Winnicott, 1971a, p. 91). Only thus was I able to relieve her of the unconscious dread that nobody could ever bear to be in touch with her most intense feelings – as they had been at the time of the original trauma.

As Winnicott says (1965, p. 258), this was something very different from the notion of cure by corrective emotional experience. A key distinction here is that the experience unconsciously being looked for was quite different from anything I would have prescribed for the patient. It was she who had found the analytic experience that was in the end most therapeutically effective; *it had not been provided for her.* But what had been provided was a sufficient security in the analytic 'holding' for her to bear to remember the early trauma of not having been held; and now her remembering (by re-experiencing that trauma in the transference) could be in the presence of someone against whom she could safely rage – as at the mother who had become absent through fainting.

Much later in the analysis the patient reflected upon that time. She said of this: 'What was so important was not just that you survived: *it was that you survived – but only just.*' It had therefore been vital to her that she had seen evidence of my being truly in touch with the intensity of her distress, for it had been that which had contributed to her mother's fainting. But it had also been essential that I had managed to find a way of staying with her most difficult feelings from that trauma – that I had not deflected these by trying to be the 'better mother'.

CONCLUSION

WHEN WE ARE treating a patient who has been trauma-tized, it is inevitable that the traumatic experience will eventually come to be represented in the transference – if we do not deflect this or prevent it. The re-experiencing of trauma then turns out to be a subtle blend of truth and illusion: it combines the realities both of the analytic situation and of the patient's internal world where uncon-scious memories of trauma are still dynamically present. The resulting illusion, of the past and the present being powerfully the 'same', is based upon an unconscious set of experiences that have remained timeless – because in the unconscious there is no sense of time (Freud, 1915b, p. 187). A similar set of experiences in the present thus comes to represent the original trauma.

In learning to distinguish *the present* from *the past that spills into the present*, a patient has to find sufficient difference between the analytic relationship now and the situation as it had been at earlier times of trauma. This means that the analyst has to be careful not to be disturbingly similar to the patient's primary objects of the past; but it also turns out to be crucial that it is the patient who discovers the necessary difference – this should not be intrusively demonstrated by the analyst. Likewise, any similarity that may come to be used to represent trauma should also be found by the patient: in no way should this be deliberately introduced by the analyst.

If the analytic process is not to be impeded or distorted, the analyst has to be careful not to influence or direct the patient. This means that he should not actively provide experience that is thought to be 'good for the patient', as suggested by advocates of cure by emotional experience. But what can be provided is a security within the analytic relationship that allows the patient to feel understood, sensitively responded to and analytically 'held', by an analyst who can tolerate what is yet to come in the course of the analysis – without collapse or retaliation (Winnicott, 1971a, pp. 91 ff.).

Therefore, when a patient is prompting the analyst to depart from classical technique, particularly if it is being rigidly adhered to, this need not always be seen as seductive or manipulative. The patient may be searching for a more viable balance between the similarities in the analytic relationship (that represent trauma) and a sufficient difference that alone can provide the necessary security for the analysis to continue. It is the balance here that matters.

The patient's unconscious will find its own ways of

using the analytic encounter to represent what still
remains to be dealt with from earlier traumatic experiences. And the ways found by the unconscious are often
surprisingly different from anything that we might have
imagined, or have thought that we could devise for the
patient. As Klauber reminded us, in his first lecture (this
volume, p. 3), the transference uses reality very skilfully.

THE END OF THE ANALYSIS*   8

Nicole Berry

I F A FRIEND is going away, we rush up to him to say,
at last, all the things which we held back on the day
that we met. If someone is dying, we hurry to his
bedside to reveal the secret emotions and feelings we have
always kept to ourselves. The sense of an ending causes
us anxiety, but it also precipitates events and thoughts.
The idea that something is coming to an end makes it
more precious. The idea of death adds spice to life.
'Transience value is scarcity value in time. Limitation
in the possibility of an enjoyment raises the value of
enjoyment . . . A flower that blossoms for a single night
does not seem to us on that account less lovely,' writes
Freud (1916, pp. 305–6).

Alternatively, we can refuse to accept that anything is
ending. We can refuse to think about it: 'It is easier to
bear death when one is not thinking about it than the idea
of death when there is no danger' (Pascal, 1966, p. 72).

The idea of an analysis that never comes to an end may

* Translated from the French by David Macey.

be momentarily reassuring, but can it be sustained? It may conjure up fantasies of exhaustion or fears of being drained. These, however, are fantasies and not true realities: the unconscious can never be exhausted and thought never ends.

Can we ever write the words 'The End'?

At the end of a concert, the audience rises to its feet, but everyone can still hear a melody, notes or a theme inside their heads. Long after the holiday is over, some smell will suddenly bring back multiple images. Artists who have completed a novel, a sculpture or some other piece of work often feel an urge to create something else, as though the first piece had been no more than a sketch for something new. How can we be sure that there is such a thing as 'the last work'? One can always change the note, retouch the sketch or resolve the plot . . . differently.

Is the end of an analysis a termination? Is it a closure? Is the work all done or completed? Can we speak of 'liquidating' an analysis in the sense that we can speak of liquidating stock or reserves for which we have no use? Can we break it off as easily as we snap a piece of string? Is the end a process of separation which divides something into two different parts, each with its own clear outline? Can the Oedipus complex or a transference neurosis be 'dissolved' in the same way that a problem can be solved or resolved for life?

Is the end of the analysis a process of closure, or does it represent an opening on to something new, a sketch for a new life?

One can no more wish for the end of the analysis to come than one can hasten the process of maturation.

The analysis is coming to an end. We may feel that the end is approaching or, on the contrary, that it will never come. We may notice that we are denying that it will ever end, that we are ignoring the passage of time, that we are avoiding the words 'the end'.

'Is there such a thing as a natural end to an analysis?' asks Freud (1937a, p. 219). At some point during the treatment, this question arises for analyst and patient

alike. In an interminable analysis, it arises in a particularly cruel fashion: the very mention of 'the end' is enough to arouse feelings of rejection and helplessness or grudges which had, one thought, already been analysed. The entire imaginary field is filled with a feeling of 'nevermore', with the fear of parting and with the thought of death. The intensity of the affects which emerge may even cause the analyst to take evasive action.

Although Freud does raise the question of 'fixing a time-limit for the analysis' (1937a, p. 217), he immediately rejects the idea. Setting a time-limit does have its effects, but it is scarcely a technique to be recommended. Ferenczi (1927) also discusses the issue but concludes that the technique results in an incomplete or unfinished analysis; it means that the process of detachment cannot take place.

I would like to show that, given certain conditions, a time-limit for the analysis can be set, and to demonstrate how that device or agreement modifies the work of analysis. I would like to show that there is such a thing as the end of the analysis.

1. CRITERIA FOR THE TERMINATION OF ANALYSIS

WHILST FREUD and Ferenczi rule out the question of 'setting a time-limit', most analysts avoid the idea of the end of the analysis and psychoanalytic writings on the topic are rare. They are much more willing to discuss the ends of analysis, in other words its supposed aims.

The works of Grinberg (1980) and Gaskill (1980) seem to represent a happy compromise between the two extremes. Gaskill (1980) describes the therapeutic objectives of analysis in terms of the following criteria: capacity to love and work; ego strength; supremacy of the reality principle; understanding of inner and outer reality; dominance of the secondary process; differentiation of self and object world as a result of the processes of separation and individuation. He contrasts this evaluation in terms of objectives with the rule of 'goallessness', which corresponds more closely to our modern ideal. Grinberg's paper (1980) is critical of evaluations based upon 'criteria for termination' on the grounds that they may unwittingly lead to the construction of an analytic false self if the patient colludes in conforming to a model. He therefore sees the termination of the analysis in terms of the resolution of transference and countertransference. For Grinberg, the essential points are the analysis of separation and the giving-up of the fantasy of timelessness. The article also makes an important point as to the identity of the psychoanalyst or, rather, it seems to me, as to his function. According to Grinberg, one of the qualities required in a psychoanalyst is 'tolerance to certain kinds of frustration' (1980, p. 27). The kinds of frustration that we always talk about so vaguely are always narcissistic in origin.

2. THE END OF THE ANALYSIS AND NARCISSISM

IT IS NOT in fact possible to evaluate the desirability of terminating an analysis without looking at the changes that have taken place both in the patient and in *the analyst's ego ideal*. We must, that is, examine the analyst's subjective assessment of how the patient has changed in relation to an ideal. In other words, we must examine the narcissistic involvement of the analyst. The decision to terminate is always a compromise between the demands of reality, and in particular of the passage of time, and those of the analyst's ego ideal, of the ideal of perfectibility. This presupposes a degree of renunciation on the part of both partners. The patient's expectations of undergoing a metamorphosis prove to have been illusory; the analyst's desire to change the other proves to have been over-ambitious. As they part at the door, both analyst and patient must realize that they have changed and, at the same time, that they are what they are. Both have to become reconciled to not knowing, to accepting that knowledge has its limitations. They have to accept the secrecy that makes the other an other, and the element of the unknown within themselves. If we knew too much, we would become prisoners; there would be no more worlds to discover, either inside us or outside us.

A compromise is reached, and a possible date for termination is set. If, on the appointed day, a new path opens up, we follow it by mutual agreement. The decision has to be taken jointly.

This compromise attitude may even result in an admission of defeat, as when we are forced to conclude that the patient refuses to change, that the negative therapeutic reaction is too great or that primary masochism is predominant. We therefore have to reconsider the limitations of analysis and our own criteria for indicating analysis. We have to come to terms with our fantasies of omnipotence, with the excessive need to make reparation that leads us to accept any patient who requests analysis, regardless of his pathology or our limitations.

3. THE LIMITATIONS OF ANALYSIS

THE TENTH VOLUME of the *Nouvelle Revue de Psychanalyse* (1974) took as its theme 'Aux limites de l'analysable'. The limits as to what can or cannot be analysed constantly recede as we look for ever more archaic elements, as we tolerate 'acting out' – either interpreting it on the spot or leaving it to evolve – and as our ability to understand neutral or blank elements which would once have discouraged us increases (I am thinking here of the work of Green, 1973a and Giovacchini, 1972).

We owe our ability to read into the invisible, to see where there is nothing to be seen, to Winnicott, and it is thanks to Bion (1970) that we can glimpse existence behind the appearance of non-existence and find form in formlessness.

Freud sees the limitations of psychoanalysis in very different terms. He refers to the *adhesiveness* or viscosity of the libido, and to the depletion of plasticity, of the capacity for change (1937a, p. 241). Freud often speaks of depletion and even of wish-fulfilment as a 'reduction to zero'. Personally, I tend to see this as a fantasy: the idea of drying up or draining the Zuyder Zee may, that is, relate to a depressive fear of the breast drying up.

He also refers to the *principle of strife* (1937a, p. 246), which is bound to an element of free aggressivity. Perhaps, as Freud says, this is a hereditary element, although that is scarcely a convincing explanation, or perhaps it relates to a search for a conflict that can provide the death instinct with an outlet, or that can resolve persecution anxiety. The fact that neither a solution nor an outlet can ever be found might explain why the conflict reoccurs, why the subject actively looks for an external conflict to resolve internal tensions.

The *bedrock* of penis envy in women and of the struggle against passive attitudes in men (1937a, p. 252) appears to me to be crumbling away. Melanie Klein has shown that penis envy and the desire to have a child can be analysed as a desire for an inexhaustible breast. In the present socio-cultural climate, moreover, men find it easier to come to terms with passive attitudes; social changes have given such unconscious tendencies a new value. At the same time, the virile business woman is highly respected.

If we think of the pathology of so-called borderline states, which I would prefer to describe as 'borderless states', the bedrock is in fact the analyst, who stands firm in the face of the patient's tempestuous desires and demands. He is the reality against which the storm breaks. Whatever happens, he is still the analyst. I refer, in other words, to what Georges Favez (1974) terms the 'resistance of analysis'. 'For the analyst, the most important thing is to go on being an analyst.' The bedrock is made up of the limitations imposed upon the boundless greed of some patients, of the ego's capacity to master that greed and to find other sources of satisfaction. The possibility of terminating the analysis is determined by the establishment of limits, and those limits are internal.

MELANIE KLEIN (1950) definitely takes an intrapsychic view of the matter. The decision to terminate an analysis presupposes that the ego has acquired the capacity to synthesize, that splitting has diminished and that the aggressive and libidinal desires have come closer together because hate has been tempered by love. For Klein, the termination of an analysis is in the nature of a weaning experience. The child experiences its loss as resulting from its hate and greed. Hence the vital need for an adequate analysis of the conflicts of the first year of life.

It is precisely when this weaning experience is impossible, when the patient wants to possess the analyst completely and permanently that the temptation to set time-limits may arise. Greed gives the analyst a feeling of being invaded and the transference resistance – in other words, the demand for love and satisfaction – becomes an obstacle to the work of analysis and provokes a feeling of incompetence and impotence. Although spatial limits have been set to ensure that the analytic framework is respected and to prevent actions from replacing words, the temporal limits always seem to retreat, as though they were indefinable. Just as the patient tries to ignore the limitations placed upon his actions, he attempts to ignore the limitations of life and forgets the passage of time.

5. THE QUESTION OF FANTASY AND REALITY

IN SUCH CASES, there can be no possibility of arriving at 'a rigid separation of reality and fantasy' (Ferenczi, 1927, p. 79), as it is impossible for the patient to give up pleasure in unconscious fantasy. According to this view, the aim of treatment appears to be 'the laying bare of the fantasy'. But in this text – and Ferenczi is thinking primarily of hysterics – fantasy is equivalent to mendacity.

THE END OF
THE ANALYSIS

106 I would like here to suggest that 'laying bare' can have
another meaning.

*Analysis can in fact be experienced as a fulfilment of
the 'family romance' of childhood.* At the level of fantasy,
the analyst is seen as an ideal parent who adopts, keeps and
loves the patient without any time-restrictions. Analysis
then becomes an ideal dream-life which compensates for
the narcissistic disappointment which lies at the origin of
the family romance. The analysis itself is cathected in
both libidinal and narcissistic terms, to the detriment of
real life.

In cases of extreme narcissistic suffering, when the
patient feels that he was not loved or recognized as a
child, the need for his identity to be recognized outweighs
his libidinal needs. So long as the patient remains
convinced that the analyst does not see him as a unique
individual, and will not remember his face, some problematic or some particular quality about their relationship –
there can be no question of the analysis being terminated.

Ferenczi's demand for the 'separation of reality and
fantasy' can have only a limited application. Psychical
reality is indeed a reality, and so is the transference
relationship. No matter whether the analyst represents
an ideal parent, a protective father or a castrating mother
to the patient, and no matter whether the patient
represents a child, a parent or an alter ego to the analyst,
a real affective relationship has been established between
them. As John Klauber writes, it is because the analysis
becomes a friendly relationship that it is detraumatized
(1981, p. 119). The relationship can then be internalized,
and the analysis can come to an end. Klauber sees
the traumatic effects of analysis as resulting from the
'disruption of the stimulus barrier against the unconscious' (1981, p. 112). Before we can interpret, we must
therefore know against what impulse the patient is strug-
gling; that knowledge derives from both logical thought
and analytic intuition.

Analysis can also have traumatic effects because of the
faithful and rigid application of rules which, for the

patient, reproduce a childhood situation in which the imperative to conform destroyed all warmth and affection. In such cases, the value of the spontaneity which meant so much to Klauber is all-important. Spontaneity results from friendship, from a positive countertransference; there is no need to suppress momentary feelings of annoyance or weariness. It is also the fruit of experience: the analyst learns how to make the patient accept rules and limitations, but at the same time he learns how to act naturally. He can be the same person in the consulting room that he is in other relationships, and he can speak equally naturally in both contexts. Patients who have had to construct a false self benefit greatly from this authenticity. Spontaneity is a mark of mutual trust and it is a quality specific to relationships developed during the end of the analysis.

As the analysis comes to an end, we have to mourn the imagos the other has incarnated, but we can still cherish the quality of the relationship, provided that it has been authentic and not merely 'scientific'. Ferenczi (1985, p. 85) compares what happens at the end of a successful analysis to two friends saying goodbye after having worked together for years. They are still friends, but they accept that a friendship at school is not a friendship for life and that they both have to develop in line with their own projects. There is nothing tragic about the scene.

6. THE END OF THE ANALYSIS AND TRANSFERENCE

JOHN KLAUBER is the author of a fine study of analyses that cannot be terminated (1981, pp. 63–73). The difficulties they pose relate to the fact that the patient finds it impossible to introject the analyst because he cannot bring together the love and hate he feels. Klauber relates this difficulty to envy, which prevents the patient from transforming the analyst's interpretations into a creative identification. Its roots lie in maternal deprivation, which results in bondage to the object. The difficulty of terminating the analysis relates to the loss of a primary love object and to a massive, ambivalent introjection of the love object.

We cannot, then, discuss the criteria for ending an analysis without referring to the transference relationship. But can we therefore speak of transference being dissolved? 'I do not want to destroy the positive feelings I have for you,' says a patient. Transference is not dissolved; it has to be worked through. But the compulsion to repeat may be dissolved. 'I no longer feel under an obligation to repeat,' says another patient.

7. ANALYSES THAT CAN BE TERMINATED

HERE IS an exchange from the end of an analysis:

'Life, life, I have a thirst for life, life.'
The patient goes on coming as regularly as ever, but he often talks to me about his plans for the future.
'I want to live my own life, to spread my wings and fly away, to go away, but you are holding me back.
I tell you that I am fine, but you just laugh at me.'
Analysis of these projections brings up the word 'parting'. The patient cannot think of parting without thinking of death. If he went away and never saw me again, I might as well be dead. Leaving me means putting me to death. Didn't his mother almost die giving birth to him?
'Yes, birth. That is precisely what I am living through.'

The end of the analysis reactivates the most archaic mechanisms, including that of projection. The patient says 'You are holding me back', whereas he is in fact 'holding back' his own desire to leave. These archaic mechanisms can, however, be analysed immediately and to good effect; they are present in all of us but, provided that the analysis has been pursued far enough, they are also mobile. Thus, the patient wants the analyst to keep him to prove that he is irreplaceable.

The end of the analysis reactivates the depressive position, which has already been worked through during the transference neurosis. This time, the terms of the equation are reversed. It is not the patient who is afraid of being abandoned; in his fantasy, it is the analyst who will be abandoned, and he will be so hurt by the loss of his object that he may die. In other words, the fears of childhood have been reactivated. If we attempt to avoid this moment or to 'speed up the process', we may lose a unique opportunity to achieve a better resolution of the depressive anxiety and of the guilt feelings that are bound up with it. *The end of the analysis is a vital moment because it sums up all the important moments in the analysis.* It is often experienced in a depressive mode, as the patient relives all the traumatic partings of childhood. He has to be able to assume two positions: that of an object suffering a loss, and that of a subject imposing an absence. If we fail to see that or if we try to speed things up – which is tantamount to avoiding the issue – we compromise all the work that has been done.

It is also *because life and death instincts come into conflict* that this moment is so important. It is a decisive moment and a choice has to be made: another inevitable failure or a new life. If we spare the patient this choice, we compromise his reasons for living. The analysis itself has to be mourned. Patient and analyst must work through, foresee and complete the work of mourning together. The work of mourning means actively recalling memories in order to succeed in a giving-up [*assumer le renoncement*], recognizing the separate identities of analyst and patient, and feeling grateful to a lost object. In terms of analysis, it means introjecting a capacity for self-observation and internalizing a capacity to tolerate a more supple superego. It means acquiring the ability to take care of oneself, as the life instinct demands, and to enjoy greater freedom at the level of fantasy. As in certain

110   cases of mourning, an increase in libido can sometimes be observed as the analysis draws to an end. Abraham writes: 'We find . . . that when the mourning person has gradually detached his libido from his dead object by means of the "work of mourning" he is aware of an increase in his sexual desires' (1924, p. 473). The increase in libido to be observed as the analysis comes to an end can take the sublimated form of a desire to take the initiative or to extend one's intellectual interests.

'I have a new appetite for life.'

'I wouldn't like to just walk out and slam the door.'

It is not that the patient is still afraid of his aggressive instincts. It is rather that he is using a form of negation to say that he would like to avoid having to go through the door, that he would prefer not to experience the moment of parting, that he wants to avoid the sorrow and the pain of leaving.

When I point this out, he thinks, 'It is painful for both of us.'

The sorrow and the pain of leaving an empty space, of casting aside a book that has been read too often. Whenever this man had to leave a woman he loved – or wanted to leave her – his fear of causing a woman pain, of hurting her and of seeing her die reappeared. These fantasies screened the guilt he felt about hurting his mother when he was born, about leaving her, about being a demanding child, about being a burden to her. As a result of these conflicting feelings, he seduced one woman after another, left them all and then took up with them again.

It is no clinical accident that I should choose to write this passage. The place left by this patient is not empty; it is taken up with the article I am writing. Without knowing it, he left me a gift – the pleasure of the work I bear within me – and my pleasure reminds me of his: 'I greatly enjoyed making a woman pregnant.'

The patient is thinking of what will happen after the analysis. Perhaps one day he will write something for one of the journals he sometimes sees lying around in my office. That would be one way of not leaving me, of course, but it might also be a way of taking my place, or even of outdoing me. At the same time, it would be a way of continuing the analysis, of making a relationship that has ended live on in the written word. The aggressive desire to dominate an analyst who represented the powerful figures he envied as a child is bound up with the libidinal pleasure of the transference. The destructive desire is giving way to an internalization of our relationship, of the work we accomplished together. His positive feelings are no longer split off from his negative feelings.

The patient stops and thinks. He becomes conscious of an old fantasy: a butterfly is about to take wing, leaving its cocoon behind like a cast-off.

If he walked out slamming the door, would he escape my anger?

'Yes,' says the patient. 'I could never imagine how anyone could be happy if they let someone go and saw them leading their own life.' For a long time, we concentrate on working through our parting and the rejection it implies.

'You are a soul-sister,' he says as he arrives for the next session '. . . a hook. You become hooked, and the hook tears into you when you want to leave' [The play is on âme soeur and hameçon – Tr.]. The ambivalence can be assumed via an analysis of the wish to be rejected, the fear of retaliation and the contradictory wish to keep a soul-sister and at the same time to get off the hook. The patient alternates between wanting to leave and wanting to stay, and thus re-enacts his relations with his mother and with other women, the internal conflict between his regressive desire to remain in his cocoon and his aggressive desire to escape it. The way in which he alternates between the two positions also screens a sado-masochistic conflict between a desire to dominate and a desire to submit, to keep and to reject, to cling to the object and to be free of it.

The end of the analysis provides a unique opportunity to analyse these alternating positions 'in the here and

THE END OF
THE ANALYSIS

now'. Because only a single person and a single place are involved, the conflicting instincts can come together.

The separation that occurs at the end of the analysis reactivates the depressive position, and analysis of the splitting of the libidinal instincts leads to an increased desire to live and an increased capacity to make reparation. Throughout the analysis, the patient unconsciously wanted to conform to his analyst's desires, and his desire has now been transformed into a wish to take care of her. She is tired. Does she lead an active life? Does she really breathe in life?

Klauber's reference to envy (1981, p. 71) seems to me to be rather narrow. If interpretations are to be transformed into a creative identification, the patient's envy must have been analysed and must have given way to gratitude. But we must also take into account the patient's own instinctual *élan*, which allows him to overcome the pain of separation and to begin the process of creative reparation: he too can care for others, write, build, draw, etc. Envy can take on different qualities, and it gradually evolves into gratitude. It is not a feeling of 'all or nothing', of 'for or against'. We can encounter various different forms of envy: destructive, hateful envy; envy that gives rise to rancour, with all the pleasures involved in rancour and the rationalizations upon which it feeds; envy which is experienced as fascination, and which immobilizes the subject and wards off destruction; envy tinged with sorrow, which does not seek to destroy the object, but tries to retain it in order to contemplate and enjoy its sorrow via a process of introjective identification; sympathetic envy based upon loving introjective identification.

Analysis takes the patient through certain of these different gradations and affective tonalities of envy, and finally allows him to cathect real life. At that point, the patient can take his leave.

I agree that the emphasis has to be placed upon the analysis of the splitting of feelings, and that aggressivity is usually the repressed pole. No one can stand on his or

her own two feet or enjoy a feeling of inner security while
being angry or envious. As Freud writes (1937a, p. 238):
'The therapeutic effect depends on making conscious
what is repressed, in the widest sense of the word, in the
id.' And as Edmund Gosse writes (1907, p. 164) of a
particularly bitter experience of disappointment: 'There
is a limit to endurance, and with a sense of having been
torn by the tooth of ingratitude, I fled . . . never to return.'
Hate and the need for vengeance gradually fade away.

Although parting may imply a desire to destroy the
object and to abandon or reject it as though it were
something inert, in my view it is more usually bound up
with the destruction of the object in Winnicott's (1968)
sense of the term. The destruction of the object creates
the quality of externality. The analyst may be destroyed
in fantasy, but neither the real person nor the object
relation is destroyed. As Winnicott demonstrates, the
destruction of the object in fantasy externalizes it and
makes it possible for the partners to separate. In that
sense, reality is severed from fantasy, as Ferenczi (1927)
would have it. There is a vital distinction between the
destruction characteristic of the depressive phase and the
destruction of an object that has been used. If the patient
remained fixated in the depressive position, his thoughts
would be fixated on the damaged object and on an endless
attempt to repair it. Separation must therefore take place
if thought is to spread its wings and to enjoy full mobility.
Being separated from the object is an essential precondition for the emergence of creative thought.

The fact that separation occurs in fantasy does not
mean that it is not real. A day and an hour must be set
for saying goodbye; otherwise, the door is still open and
it is still possible to go back. The separation must be real
if its 'occurrence' is to be analysed.

Certain psychoanalytic societies adhere to the rule that
analysts under supervision should remain in analysis for
a period of years, or at least see this as desirable. But
doesn't this encourage them to avoid the issue of separation? When Goethe's Wilhelm Meister had completed

his apprenticeship, he left his parents and his teachers. Shouldn't the analyst do the same?

9. INTERNALIZATION OF THE RELATIONSHIP AND DISENGAGEMENT OF THE EGO*

SEPARATION IMPLIES the emergence of two distinct identities in both fantasy and reality. But the imaginary relationship lives on inside the subject: he talks to himself as he once talked to his analyst, and perceives that the demands he attributed to his analyst were in fact his own demands, that it was he himself who kept insisting that he should make more effort and struggle harder against his 'weaknesses'. As he internalizes a superego which is less strict, relationships between the agencies become more supple. As the guilt which forced him to remember lessens, he becomes freer in relation to himself and more detached from his memories. The relationship with the analyst has allowed him to open up wider internal spaces. The self no longer clings to the superego. The patient is now his own 'container', in Bion's sense of the word. He can therefore discover various ways of distancing himself and of accepting the unknown. As Bion demonstrates, this notion of distance relates to the depressive position. I would add that *patience* is also involved. Whereas the

---

* The mechanism of disengagement [*dégagement*] is related to the mechanisms used by the ego to regulate tension. Lagache (1986, p. 271) refers initially to the work of Bibring and to the distinction between defence mechanisms and working off mechanisms: 'The concept therefore corresponds to the realization of possibilities open to the subject; resolution of the defensive conflict is a necessary but not a sufficient condition for *dégagement*.' Lagache evokes a revival of vitality and of consciousness supported by the indestructible structures that are revived and activated by transference. He compares the mechanism with Balint's 'new beginning'. The manifest creativity of the analysand cannot be stirred unless it is awakened by the silent creativity of the psychoanalyst, who watches over him as a mother watches over her child's first steps (1986, p. 274).

search for facts or for proof, and paranoid-schizoid memories both justify and feed feelings of persecution, *depressive thought is contemplative.* It allows the organization of fantasies, and it is precisely this that we observe at the end of the analysis. Whereas persecutory words constantly re-echo through our heads, depressive thought can tolerate silences and arrange harmonies.

10. THE REVIVAL OF INSTINCTS

A S A R E S U L T of the reactivation of the instincts which I mentioned earlier, analytic activity becomes intense. *Now that the end of the analysis is in sight, instincts are revived.* Whereas regression is common at the beginning of an analysis, we now see a progression. The patient has at last learnt to trust someone, to let go, and now he begins to take both his life and his analysis into his own hands. The sessions become remarkably dense. Not a minute is lost, and the thread is taken up from one session to the next. Old material reappears with new associations, and it is worked into a broader picture. The material, affects and thought all become *concentrated.* I would describe this intense moment as 'a process of termination'. It is the source of immense pleasure.

My answer to Freud's question, 'Is there such a thing as a natural end to an analysis?' would be 'Yes', provided that the end is both foreseen and analysed.

Freud (1937a, p. 216) associates the end of the analysis with Rank's theory of the trauma of birth.

The patient entered analysis in the expectation of undergoing a metamorphosis, but has had to give up the fantasy of being transformed by an all-powerful analyst. Just as we patiently worked through the patient's history, the transference and the fantasies it screened, we now have to analyse the experience of parting. Just as being born implies being parted from the body of one's mother, so being parted from the cradle of analysis, or from its imprisoning cocoon, implies being born and emerging into the open air. Like a child, the patient leaves behind him an envelope for which he has no further use.

We had decided to terminate the analysis. My woman patient dreamed that she was taking the cushions off a divan. She saw herself as a child. She stood up and tried to walk by herself, staggering towards a table leg for support. She associates: 'I see myself as a little girl trying to walk. I have two very strong desires: I want to be independent, without anyone holding me, but I want to be a baby again.' She had never previously formulated the desire to be a baby. Presumably the danger of being trapped in my arms had to recede before she could bring herself to think of it.

'Analysis is like a placenta. I want to be separated from it very gently. I want to be alone, to get by alone. I have more energy than I could have believed possible. I can breathe properly.'

'When I came here, I was defeated, hurt and tired; you have awakened in me a powerful desire to live.'

This patient's analysis had in fact revealed an oedipal experience of death. When she was ten, her father had told her about a traumatic experience that brought him close to death as though he were telling a secret they had to keep to themselves. As a result, her life was dominated by a suffocating feeling of guilt. The feeling that she had to make reparation became an unconscious 'argument' in favour of continuing the oedipal relationship, and her account of it was highly eroticized. As she talked about it in analysis, the old relationship gradually became libidinized. The notion of being her mother's rival appeared and revealed guilt feelings which had previously seemed to be absent. Previously, the aggressivity implicit in rivalry had been directed against the defeated, hurt woman.

'Going through analysis was like being born. I have never felt at once so young and so old. I feel young because I have a new life ahead of me, and old because of all the experience I have behind me. I am at once full of joy and full of sorrow.'

JOY AND SORROW: at the end of the analysis, the conflict between life and death instincts is reactivated, as, for example, in the temptation to regress and run away from life. 'You are holding me back,' said the first patient I discussed, as he projected his regressive desires on to me. His 'negative therapeutic reaction' can be explained in terms of the reactivation of the conflict between his life instincts and his death instincts. The best possible outcome would be for the 'internal demand for work' (Pontalis, 1977, p. 241) which the instinct forces upon the psychical apparatus to provide an outlet for the conflict. As the feeling of guilt declines, work can be combined with pleasure and the binding process can be extended.

Talking about the end of an analysis means having to talk about life and death. The experience of analysis might be described as a long process of regression which removes us from the demands of time and takes us into the shelter of analytic space. Like any regression, it is accompanied by a fantasy of death and resurrection. It is normally at the end of the analysis that this fantasy finds expression. One often hears expressions such as 'turning over a new leaf', 'being reborn' or 'being someone else'. 'I was never properly born,' says a patient, and suddenly pours out the emotions he usually holds back. The fantasy of death and resurrection finds expression at the end of the analysis because it emanates from a revival of instincts.

The end of an analysis often coincides with a promise of birth: a child will be born and may replace the relationship that is about to come to an end. In analytic terms, the child has to be seen as prolonging a relationship that has run its term. Alternatively, the patient may decide to become an analyst. This may be a way of not leaving his own analyst, either in fantasy or in reality: being like him is a way of not leaving him. In the best of cases, the desire to be an analyst implies internalization of the analytic relationship.

Both these possibilities can be seen either as a denial that a break has taken place, as a happy outcome or as the replacement of fantasy by reality. Will the patient always need to have a relationship in which he can merge with someone, even when he also begins to establish more adult relationships? The fulfilment of a childhood wish may also be at stake: the girl's wish to have a baby and the boy's wish to be a father, and the various possibilities must also be analysed in that register. Every desire we ever experience stems from that childhood wish. All these possibilities represent a happy compromise between the conflicting life and death instincts.

12. THE SITE OF THE ANALYSIS

THE PATIENT leaves his analyst because their relationship has been internalized. The analysis comes to an end because it lives on in the patient. And what can we say about the place where the analysis took place? Like the house in which we were born, and like a baby's inanimate environment, the place in which the analysis took place is narcissistically cathected (Berry, 1982). The baby's environment provides it with a narcissistic support and makes its mother's absence bearable. When a patient leaves his analyst, he also leaves the place in which the analysis unfolded, and that is often particularly painful. Long after he has forgotten the analyst's face, he will still recall the image of a house, of an office or of some familiar detail that became dear to him. 'I still think of your little office up there, and of other people going into it,' a woman patient wrote to me when she had completed her analysis. My office is not dead; it has not been forgotten. And nor is it neutral. A dream this patient recounted in our last session explains what she felt after we parted. She came into my office, feeling rather sad, and saw some prints on the wall. They were all very beautiful, and they depicted foetuses. For her, my office was a place of birth and a source of creativity. The prints were associated with what went on there. Her fantasy was of course a way of making reparation for the depression she felt.

Unlike the image of a cocoon that is left empty and inert, the fantasy of a space that is lived in and which goes on living provides an image of an analyst to whom reparation has been made, with the space acting as a metaphor for a person. At the same time, it is the object of a separate narcissistic cathexis.

13. TIME AS CONTAINER

THE ANALYST was a container, in Bion's sense of the term, for the patient's affects and emotions. The container is not displaced on to a setting or a place, but on to the psyche itself: the patient is now capable of experiencing and containing his affects. He can do so because he is now situated within time, whereas he once lived in a fantasy of timelessness. He has a past in which he can recognize himself, a present which does not drown him, and a future in which he can situate his projects, and cathect, transform and sublimate his affects. St Augustine once asked if we mentally foresee events that have yet to occur in terms of pre-existing images. This is precisely what happens at the end of the analysis, when the patient talks to his analyst about his plans for the future. Personal time becomes a new space: *time becomes a container for the patient's psyche*. Because he has become conscious of elements that were repressed, his psychic space opens up. It is no longer bounded by the compulsive need to remember, the need not to forget, for example, the parent he once wanted to drive away. As he becomes more able to cathect himself narcissistically, it becomes possible for him to integrate past, present and future, and to locate himself with a temporal continuum. It is probably impossible to represent time without using images, which can be either linear, circular or three-dimensional. A year becomes an image of someone standing on a line, inside an imaginary circle, or of someone contained within a three-dimensional solid.

We can use a variety of images to represent various kinds of time.

– When the subject proceeds from idea to act [*passage à l'acte*], will not tolerate frustration or cannot wait, we experience a linear form of time. The patient moves in linear fashion from wish to wish-fulfilment; refusals and frustrations merely intensify the need for satisfaction. No other desire can emerge, and no other outcome (sublimation or displacement) is possible. The refusal to tolerate frustration corresponds to a linear conception of time.

– Unlimited time. The patient feels that his thoughts are lost in time, and that he himself is floating. Bion (1970) notes that if projection is to take place, space must be limited; if it is not, emotion will be experienced as being lost. Anzieu (1985) also demonstrates the need for a narcissistically cathected 'envelope of well-being' which he describes as constituting an 'ego skin'.

– In cases of disavowal or denial, time is experienced as a break, as a process of folding or splitting. When a person is split, there is no continuity. Each part is split off and exists in its own time, oblivious to the existence of other parts.

– In persecution, time is repetitious and narrow. Memories come back, and they are always the same. They harass the subject and imprison him in a cell where his thoughts are no more than noises that reverberate around him.

– The punctiform time of hallucinations and of fascination. Visual satisfaction is the only possible form of satisfaction. The moment of the initial encounter is more highly cathected than the brief liaison that follows. We can find many examples in literature, as in Thomas Mann's *Tonio Kröger*, or Dickens's *Great Expectations* or *Little Dorrit*.

If a patient opts for hallucination, for the fascination of an ideal object or the illusory satisfaction of what is

'already there', the whole of time is concentrated into a
single moment.

The expression 'taking one's time' expresses this form of satisfaction better than 'having time', which is closer to the idea of leisure.

– At the end of the analysis, time should be something leisurely. Choices can be made and time expands into a broad surface. Thoughts too have room to expand; the capacity to tolerate frustration allows the patient's thoughts to roam in various directions. Conversely, as Winnicott shows, thought allows one to tolerate frustration, not only because it brings the object of desire into the present, but also because thought itself is a source of pleasure, because of the pleasure of thought, the pleasure of thinking.

Thought presupposes negation and the possibility of changing objects. The analyst is not the object of the patient's desire and, if his thoughts are mobile, he can seek satisfaction elsewhere. The analyst must therefore keep up the level of frustration by respecting the rule of non-intervention and thus giving the patient cause for thought.

– When the patient can accept frustration, he can direct his gaze elsewhere, and his space and time can expand. He is not imprisoned by his desire to possess the analyst, to prevent the analyst going away. Both analyst and patient have their own space, and they live their lives in their own time-continuum.

In conclusion, we can then say that *the patient's time is a container for his desires, his emotions and his thoughts.* His memory contains the past, and time contains both the desires projected into the future, the desires he has relinquished and the desires he sustains. The past is contained within his memory. His memories are possessions, but he can let them go without feeling too guilty or too anxious.

The links the analyst makes through his interpretations connect moments that are far removed from one another in time, and they help time to become a container for the patient. On the other hand, his refusal to interpret, his neutrality and his ability to daydream – which is similar to a mother's ability to daydream while holding her child – allow the patient to drift away into a wider space. It is in this sense that Bion's (1970) recommendation that the analyst should be 'free from memory and desire' is to be understood.

14. TIME AND SPACE

ALTHOUGH THE psyche needs a restricted space, and although the ego needs an 'envelope of well-being' or an object if it is to enter into a relationship, the perception or the fantasy of boundless space is a useful aid to creativity. Freud demonstrates the role of pleasure in stimulating intellectual activity. Fairbairn (1952) insists upon the primacy of the object, on the primacy of 'object-seeking' over 'pleasure-seeking'. I would agree with him, but I associate Fairbairn with the hills of Scotland, with the vast, empty sea, with a space that is not bounded by any horizon and which merges into the luminous mist and the sky. Human beings need boundaries and walls, but they also need space and emptiness. 'There is nothing but reality outside the door. The only hope for light comes from the window, from the sunrise, from the horizon', wrote Milena Jesenská (1985, p. 118). In order to create, we have to empty, as opposed to being invaded by anxiety, persecution or even desire. If we are to create, we must have the space of indefinite time, the space of a silent time that is available for new cathexes. The mists of time are a source of anxiety, but they can also stimulate the imagination. The harsh shadows cast by the sun can be reassuring, but as night falls they become blurred and difficult to see, and that too can be a source of enchantment. Our thoughts can roam free and go in search of the unknown as boundless space merges with boundless time.

The end of the analysis may mean acceptance of the unknown. When we set a date for our last meeting, the future is both predictable and unknown. Fixing a time-limit means agreeing to cut ourselves off from memories, from the past, from a familiar world. How does this process of detachment come about?

Although analysis of the transference allows the patient to break off relations with his analyst, and to free himself of the oedipal guilt that binds him to the past, and from the paralysing need to make reparations, his fantasies still have a hold over his thoughts. Can freedom of thought ever be complete? Are we ever free of our unconscious fantasies?

15. FANTASIES OF BEING ATTRACTIVE AND THE ATTRACTIONS OF FANTASY

BECAUSE he wants to be recognized and loved, the patient tells a story designed to make him attractive to his analyst. A distinction can be made between *two levels of working through in analysis.*

Working through and reconstructing the patient's story gives him a sense of identity which can be sustained through various events, attitudes and identifications. This is what I term the 'primary romance' (Berry, 1979). The reconstruction which emerges as memories return, and as gaps are filled in, constitutes *the manifest content of the analysis.* As Winnicott and Grinberg remind us, we must, however, also take into account the way in which the patient colludes in playing the game expected of him by the analyst. Collusion during reconstruction may reflect the influence of the 'false self'. Normally, the reconstruction of a story has an important narcissistic function: it helps the patient in the work of separation and individuation. He becomes a container for his own history, and the owner of his own time. He can therefore recognize himself as an individual, as distinct from his analyst, provided that the latter does not encroach upon his discoveries.

For both partners, working through is based upon a desire to know; it cannot occur unless that instinctual element is present. Working through also presupposes the ability to wait, and the anticipation of the pleasure of knowing.

As the patient tells his story, he alternates between making affirmations and then denying what he has affirmed. This is due to the power of repression, and it frustrates the ego's desire to know. But the repetitions, the scattered details and the discrepancies between his thoughts signal the existence of a *latent content*, in other words the existence of a whole fantasy organization. Discovering this is the greatest of all pleasures. As Freud observes, 'We have only a single clue to start from – though it is a clue of the highest value – namely, the antithesis between the primary and the secondary processes' (1937a, p. 225). The antithesis is signalled by discrepancies, errors, slips of the tongue, denials and various modes of thought. Thus, we have the event; the story of that event; the story as it is worked through, with its associations and various historical moments; the emotional experience of telling the story; the fantasy that lies behind the story.

We are struck by the disparate elements, incongruous attitudes, odd details and 'bizarre objects' (Bion) which stand out because they are at odds with the story as a whole. Gradually, they come together in the mind of the analyst, and finally they acquire a certain *coherence*.

16. 'FANTASYING': THE PATIENT'S THEORY

A PATIENT who has just gone through a period of boredom and discouragement arrives for his session in a very good mood. For the first time since he began analysis, he has dreamed of having full sexual relations. He was with a married couple he knew. He wanted the woman, and was about to throw her on to a bed when her angry husband intervened and threw him out. He then found himself in a corridor with a very young girl. He began to fondle her; she was willing, but a maid interrupted them.

He took no notice, locked the door and succeeded in penetrating the girl with great pleasure.

The patient's associations relate to his day-to-day life, and he strays away from the dream content.

As so often with this patient, I feel frustrated and even annoyed by his attitude, which I resent as an interruption. I always have to pick up the thread from one session to the next; he always forgets what he has said. I think to myself, 'He really is out of reach.'

Then I mention the triangular situation at the beginning of his dream and tell him that this is new, that he has never before dreamed or thought about being in a triangle. His associations refer to relations with his mother. In the manifest story, his father is either away from home or standing on the landing, waiting for his wife to come to bed.

'What about the maid?' 'Yes,' says the patient, 'she might be you.'

The next day, he is very depressed. He is good for nothing, worthless. He will never be anything. He is angry with me because I have ruined the euphoria of the previous day.

From one session to the next, the patient alternates between euphoria and depression, and he often complains of having migraine. He always brings up a lot of interesting material, especially dreams, and he usually introduces his associations by saying, 'I don't know if . . .'

The migraines, the similarity between his depression and that of his mother, the 'I don't know if . . . ' and the difficulty he has in making associations, with the fear of 'closeness' ['*des rapprochements*'], as he puts it, begin to come together in my mind.

The patient lived for long periods with his mother, whose moods swung from depression to hyperactivity. When his father was away, he shared her bed, comforted her and listened to her. The twin themes of a heroic father and a dependent, devalorized father compromised all his identifications. The way in which his mother rationalized the depression that affected her ever since he was born leads him to think that she almost died giving birth to him.

During the early years of the analysis, memories of a highly eroticized relationship with his mother reappeared, together with the obvious denial that any sexual element had been involved. His 'I don't know if . . . ' found expression in the indirect question, 'I don't know if I really penetrated my mother.' It then became clear why he avoided associations or 'connections' based upon my interpretations: he could not draw close to the possibility [se rapprocher au risque] of the guilt associated with incestuous penetration, but there was no father to forbid incest.

As he told the story of his life, he realized that he had always refused to succeed. The same thing happened in analysis, as was obvious from the sequence of the sessions. He must not 'go too far'. The phrase always took the form of a commentary, and I mentally associated it with the dead child theme. 'Going too far' meant penetrating his mother, and perhaps giving her a child. Either the child or the mother had to die. He therefore could not fertilize the analysis, and had to avoid making connections between one session and the next.

This patient made me live through his analysis as though it were a series of acts of coitus interruptus. The preliminaries were fascinating, but some interruption always put an end to everything. He aroused me into a more active attitude than usual; the passive homosexual attitude was a defence against the guilty oedipal attitude. He took an obvious pleasure in this. I represented a potent father, but our relationship was sterile. The interpretations I tried to put forward therefore had no lasting effect. We had to work through the implicitly destructive attitude conveyed by the derisive image in his dream: the maid could not prevent him from fulfilling his wish.

The satisfaction I experienced with this patient was of a purely intellectual order. He suggested a theory to me, or planted a seed in me [mis graine; a pun on migraine –

Tr.], but only in an intellectual sense. Ours was a purely
intellectual relationship.

The pleasure – initially my pleasure, but also that of
the patient when he began to make his own connections
– derived from the increasing coherence or *condensation*
of the material. It was similar to the pleasure afforded by
a joke, but it lasted longer and was more fertile.

As the analysis draws to an end, the material becomes
more concentrated and the analytic process speeds up.
One feels an urgent need to understand, a certain density
and a very specific pleasure. One finds oneself thinking,
'That session was worth months of painful work.'
Presumably, the pleasure comes from the ego's increasingly supple ability to handle the material as it becomes
disengaged from the mechanisms of repression. For my
own part, I believe that it is primarily associated with the
emergence of coherence.

Freud does not mention the criterion of *coherence*, but
in 'Analysis terminable and interminable' (1937a, p. 225)
the recurrent question of how to 'tame' the instincts
produces an astonishing association: 'We can only say
"So muss denn doch die Hexe dran!" – the Witch Metapsychology. Without metapsychological speculation and
theorizing – *I had almost* said "fantasying" – we shall
not get another step forward' (*So muss* . . . 'We must call
the Witch to our help after all!' Goethe, *Faust*, my
emphasis). This is the first time that theorizing and
fantasying have been juxtaposed in this way. Although
fantasy is a derivative of the unconscious which holds
back thought, Freud gives it a truly astonishing status:
fantasying gives meaning to mental activity. Whereas
'sudden ideas' have to be interpreted in terms of a wider
body of material, the 'fantasying' which Freud evokes
here provides a theory relating to several fantasies all of
which find expression in mental activities: sowing doubts
('I don't know if . . .'), the transference relationship
(avoiding connections, stimulating activity on the part of
the psychoanalyst), repetitive, symptomatic behaviour
designed to result in failure (not going too far, in other

words failing), and apparently unrelated fantasies (a dead or depressed mother, a dead child). *The patient's unconscious desire and his defence against it* are condensed into *a single fantasy* ('going too far') which illustrates the transference relationship. *His fantasy is a theory* ('If I get really close to the analyst, she will die, or I will get a migraine as a punishment') in the sense that one can speak of a child having a theory of sexuality.

We speak of 'pulling ourselves together' and of 'gathering our thoughts', and we can repair damaged thoughts in the same way that we can assume our virility. In the same way, the patient's fantasy 'pulls together' apparently disparate elements. One of the characteristic features of his fantasy is a constant reference to the body ('Don't play with yourself', or 'Life is a burden', for example).

The pleasure of pulling things together can be contrasted with the fear of fragmentation which characterizes the paranoid-schizoid phase. 'Bringing together' repairs things that have been damaged by constituting a whole, a depressive image of the self, and it satisfies the instinct for knowledge by providing a theory. A theory is a set of ideas: the Greek *theorein* means 'reviewing, judging something on the basis of proofs'. *Theoreia* refers to the act of intellectual contemplation, but can also refer to the act of 'watching a festival'. By extension, it can also mean 'festival' or 'procession'. Having a theory thus means watching a procession or a group of people advancing towards a festival.

This account of the end of the analysis may seem somewhat idealistic, but it does reflect the desperate desire to grasp and experience as a totality. As we contemplate it, the set becomes coherent and organized. Fantasies are always inscribed in visual images. The activity of watching – the only independent activity that can be undertaken by a young child, once it has outgrown the stage of reflex actions – helps the subject to elaborate fantasies in the earliest months of life. Intellectual activity – from the child's blurred perception of an undifferentiated mother and breast to the mathematician's schematic diagrams –

always involves visual representations. A fantasy which
condenses repressed unconscious impulses, makes the
analytic material coherent, and therefore expresses the
patient's mental activity is similar to the 'chosen fact'
(Bion, 1970) which gives coherence to objects during
the paranoid-schizoid position. Bion compares analytic
thought to mathematical thought, which proceeds by
harmonizing sets, and cites Poincaré to the effect that
thought introduces order into apparent disorder. Freud
says something very similar: 'We know that the first step
towards attaining intellectual mastery of our environment
is to discover generalizations, rules and laws which bring
order into chaos' (1937a, p. 228).

An interesting point is this: the patient's choice of
defence mechanism is motivated by an underlying fantasy,
and it is permeated with desire. The hypothesis of an
underlying fantasy, or the discovery of such a fantasy,
represents a challenge to Freud's concept of the 'ego's
heritage'. It reveals one of the modalities whereby a
human being can become a real subject. Daydreaming is
an activity which allows us to play with our fantasies, to
work them through in a personal way. And every subject
has his own daydreams.

One wonders which fantasy activity represents analysis
for which subject: repeated coitus interruptus, bearing a
cross and enjoying it, trying to back the analyst into a
corner in order to release some inner tension . . . If we
lay bare the fantasy which gives the whole analysis its
meaning, we lay bare the pleasure derived from the
transference. And it is the interpretation of that pleasure
which introduces the economic and dynamic modifications.

17. THE PASSION FOR KNOWLEDGE

THERE IS only one factor that can remain beyond
interpretation, namely the passion for knowledge, the
passion for analysis which motivated our colleague John
Klauber. I like the humour in his reference to 'little-

130   described elements of the psychoanalytic relationship'
(1981, p. xi, my emphasis). As he notes 'It is strange . . .
that there seems to be no discussion of the effects on the
analyst of forming relationship after relationship of the
deepest and most intimate kind with patient after patient'
(1981, p. 48). He also notes that into his life 'come
a succession of intelligent, mostly personable younger
people who bring with them the breath of many different
lives', and that they feed into him 'considerable instinctual
stimulation' (1981, p. 50). We certainly have a passion
for truth, but we also have a passion for life and a taste
for intimacy. It is that which gives us the energy to think,
to write and to go on being psychoanalysts, to go on
pursuing internal dialogues with those who have left us.
It is that which allows us to mourn them.

    The increased spontaneity we experience at the end of
the analysis can, it appears to me, be explained in terms
of the heightened instinctual activity specific to that
moment. We no longer have to control pangs of disappointment, feelings of impotence or feelings of rejection,
and we can therefore be more naturally and more genuinely welcoming. As we move from the beginning of the
analysis to its end, we become closer to what we are in
real-life situations. There is no longer anything to hide;
our patients know all our defences and all our secrets.
Analysis ends with the mutual recognition of patient and
analyst, and with their recognition of reality.

Daniel Widlöcher

NOWADAYS IT SEEMS that people applying for psychoanalytic treatment put forward their wish for a better understanding of themselves rather than the desire to eliminate their symptoms only. These are no longer regarded as a foreign body – contrasted with an ideal self-representation – but as an expression of a lack of coherence of the self itself. My feeling is that some ten years ago patients were concerned above all with relief from symptoms, and were anxious to maintain the rather coherent image they had of themselves.

Schematically, two types of analytic demand may thus be distinguished. I would call neurotic a demand for the suppression of symptoms with, explicitly or implicitly, a request for the preservation of the previous self-image. By contrast, a demand which emphasizes a wish to improve the coherence of the self-image without really questioning the existence of any abnormal behaviour can be called narcissistic. In the first case, the demand is for change, in the second for understanding. Confronted with the first type of demand, the task of the analyst is to make clear that there is no symptomatic relief without a change in self-representation. Confronted with the second type of demand, the task is to make clear that there is no true progress in self-knowledge without change.

The so-called widening scope of psychoanalysis, the fact that more and more psychoanalysts are dealing with borderline or narcissistic disorders and character neurosis, partly justifies this evolution. Feelings of emptiness, depersonalization anxieties, alterations in reality-testing and paranoid ideas are experienced as threatening the integrity of the self rather than realized as symptoms as such. But this shift in psychopathology is not a sufficient explanation. It seems that people expect more of psychoanalysis than a simple treatment of symptoms. A better knowledge of the final goals of psychoanalytic treatment probably plays a role. But we must, ultimately, take into consideration a deeper change in the sociological representation of psychoanalysis, as well as in the expectations of patients that I have mentioned. Suppression of precise symptoms is less the aim than the more ambitious aspiration towards integrity of the self and authenticity in interpersonal communication. The narcissistic demand appears as a *fait de société* [fact of society], and psychoanalysis is considered more as a humanistic experience than a simple treatment. People are more concerned about the achievement of personality than with the normality of their behaviour.

The success of the concept of self is not irrelevant to this shift in expectations.

The concept of self is generally considered to be a complement of the concept of ego, and it is assumed that it clarifies the functions of the ego and determines its limits. But it would be necessary, to achieve those goals, for the concept of self to be related to a specific part of mental activity, itself clearly determined. It seems, on the contrary, that this concept is used in a rather vague way, and on a more intuitive than rational basis, as if it were

self-explanatory. In his editorial introduction to 'On
narcissism: an introduction', Strachey (In Freud, 1914, p. 70) states that we have to distinguish, in Freud's writings, between two different meanings of the term ego. He writes: 'At first [Freud] used the term without any great precision, as we might speak of the "self", but in his latest writings he gave it a very much more definite and narrow meaning.' So it is because it can be used 'without any great precision' that the word self is opposed to the ego. And in order to keep a 'narrow meaning' to the concept of ego, we would have to add a concept with a broader and less precise meaning. The concept of self would have the advantage of referring to a basic and common intuition, and therefore of authorizing divergent interpretations and definitions of its content. In this case, however, one would expect psychoanalysts to use it in a rather limited way, and so, by contrast, to use the concept of ego more precisely. The concept of self would be a borderland concept in psychoanalytic theory.

On the contrary, this concept is utilized more and more. Psychoanalysts use it in the understanding of the mental apparatus, pathological conditions and the technique of treatment. We are no longer aiming to complete structural differentiation by a more general concept that would help us to give a more accurate definition of the ego. For many authors, the goal now seems to be to add to the structural differentiation a precise concept that deals with a different level of the personality. But if it seems necessary to many psychoanalysts to use this concept of self, they do so in different ways and many divergent points of view are evident. Schematically we may contrast those who treat the self as being akin to the personality as a whole with those who make the self an object. Guntrip's point of view is a good example of the first theoretical orientation, which, obviously, follows Jung's line of thought in opposing the ego as subject of consciousness, and taking the self as expression of the personality. Winnicott's views follow the same trend. Asked by his French translator to delineate the distinctions he made between the concepts of self and ego, he responded: 'For me the self, which is not the ego, is the person who is me, who is only me, who has a totality based on the operation of the maturational process' (Winnicott, 1971b). The common feature of those theoretical approaches is not only the person as a whole, but the dynamic process that ensures the identity of the person. To the structural differentiation based on intersystemic conflicts is opposed, on a different level, the unity of the person based on a unique force.

From the opposite point of view, the self is considered as the object of narcissistic investment. This is exactly what Freud had in mind, in *The Ego and the Id* (1923, p. 30), when he wrote: 'When the ego assumes the features of the object, it is forcing itself, so to speak, upon the id as a love object and is trying to make good the id's loss, saying: "Look, you can love me too. I am so like the object." '

Hartmann (1950) and Hartmann, Kris and Loewenstein (1946) distinguish the self-representation from the ego. Two arguments sustain this viewpoint: the necessity of disengaging the function of a mental structure from any kind of anthropomorphic meaning; and the necessity of opposing the adaptive goal of such a structure to its narcissistic investment. In the same way many authors prefer to use the concept of self-representation rather than that of an autonomous self (Sandler, Holder and Meers, 1963). But others have a more ambiguous position, the self-object shifting in such an autonomous structure (Kohut, 1971).

It is noticeable that this shift from a self-object to an autonomous self-structure is very similar to the ambiguity regarding the concept of ego: between the ego as representation of the personality as a whole and the ego as a particular agency of the mental structure. So the confusion about the concept of self is perhaps the consequence of this ambiguity in ego theory rather than something helping to clarify it. And the different theories regarding the self are related, explicitly or implicitly, to the contradictions we can recognize in the theory of the ego.

So we wonder whether the concept of self is really a borderland concept with regard to structural differentiation and the concept of the ego? Whether it deals with a part of the mental apparatus that this differentiation does not explain? Do we have to develop a theory of the self from the theory of the ego, as Hartmann thought? Or do we have to complete the classical structural theory by means of a new and different viewpoint? The last point implies that the so-called classical theory does not explain some psychoanalytic data, and it is obvious that the major contributions to the theory of the self deal with the experience of atypical pathological structures (schizoid phenomena, narcissistic disturbances and borderline conditions).

J.-B. Pontalis (1975) raises the question: 'Is the self exportable?' It does indeed seem that an important part of the success of the concept is related to its semantic connotation. In English the word 'self' immediately suggests the idea of identity and the person. In French there are no equivalent implications, and the word '*soi*' is not used to form all the reflexive pronouns, but only the third person singular, and only in the case of an undetermined subject. This is the reason why, in the first French translation of *The Ego and the Id*, it was decided to translate the word '*Es*' by the French '*soi*'. Later, this word was replaced by the term '*ça*', that is, by a demonstrative one. But, inversely, translating '*Ich*' (ego) as '*moi*', French authors used a term that has not only the function of the first person pronoun, but also the functions of attribute and complement, giving it the meaning of an object, and facilitating its transformation into a substantive; defining the person as a whole, and thus coming very close to the meaning of the English word 'self'.

Thus, using the term '*moi*' for '*Ich*' (ego), the French translators of Freud took the risk of assimilating the psychoanalytic concept to a very traditional philosophical one. Of course, psychoanalysts took care to state a difference; but the identity of words exerted an obvious influence, and it was for this reason that Hartmann, Kris

136   and Loewenstein (1946) opposed the metaphorical and anthropomorphic influence of the French on the Freudian structural viewpoint. Although it is unnecessary to delineate this semantic difference in any more detail, it obviously explains an important misunderstanding.* In French, then, we should keep the English word 'self', to avoid any confusion with the French '*soi*'.

Many French authors argue against the necessity of individualizing this concept. They fear a recurrence of a psychology of the person – as opposed to the psychoanalytic structural theory – and think there is no need to suppress the ambiguity that characterizes the Freudian concept of ego. They even state that this ambiguity is the very core of the concept. Lagache (1961), for example, objects to a too critical view of anthropomorphism. It is, indeed, dangerous to attribute to the ego the role of the subject, as did academic psychology and phenomenology; but the ego, as a partial structure of mental life, is constituted by the internalization of interpersonal relationships. That is, the activities of the ego consist partly in a reproduction of other people's attitudes, and are the result of an identification with an alter ego. Through consciousness, the ego recognizes in itself those internalized attitudes and considers itself as an object. Lagache also makes the distinction between a subject-ego and an object-ego, sometimes fused, sometimes distinct, thanks to a process of objectivation. For Laplanche (1970), though the ego is a partial structure of the mind, its function is to represent the person as a whole. According to Freud's 'Project for a scientific psychology' (1985), he states, the fundamental characteristic of the

* Lacan's theory is probably one of the most demonstrable instances of this misunderstanding. Reducing the concept of ego to the concept of narcissistic object, Lacan emphasizes one pole of the ego concept. Keeping to this function of representation – corresponding to the myth of Narcissus watching his own image in the mirror – he points out its illusory role. The ego, as an imaginary envelope, would be the cause of failing to recognize the formations of the unconscious (see Lacan, 1966a).

ego is not adaptation to external reality but the capacity
to bind representations together. Thus a coherent system
of representations that inhibits wish-fulfilling halluci-
natory representations is created. From the genetic point
of view, Laplanche states that the libido, moving from an
external object to self-representation, invests a system of
representations related to a binding activity. So the ego
is the result of the narcissistic investment of self-representation; and it is the self-representation that constitutes
this binding activity, defining the functions of the ego as
a partial structure of the psychic apparatus.

J.-B. Pontalis (1975, p. 286) expounds, a very similar
point of view. We should not discriminate the ego,
characterized by its functions, from a self, characterized
by a system of representations. The ego is closely related
to narcissism: 'The main function of the ego is to pretend
to represent the trends of the person as a whole and to
be considered as the autonomous subject, denying its
dependent relations.'

These statements do not really diverge from a theory
of the self: the ambiguity of the concept of ego is clearly
recognized, but it is not felt necessary to suppress it by
individualizing a new concept. The advantage of such an
ambiguity would be to demonstrate that the functions of
the ego cannot be separated from the self, and that it
would be a mistake, by individualizing the concept of
the self, to reduce the concept of the ego to a trivial
psychological concept, appropriate only to adaptative
functions and cognitive skills. A more controversial issue,
from this point of view, is the close link of the self
with the ego functions. It is so evident that the self-
representations that crystallize a set of representations
are the only factor that builds the basis of the ego. It is
this issue that I would now like to discuss.

When, in the course of a psychoanalytic treatment, we
refer to the ego, we deal with a set of mental activities
that lead to a feeling of coherence and identity. So, we
speak of a cohesive system of self-representations. But

does this mean that the self constitutes an autonomous psychic reality that could be perceived by the ego, in the same way that it perceives external reality? To recognize the existence of an independent self means we forget that it is the activity of the ego that ensures the coherence of bound psychic activities. Perhaps it is a mistake to mix together the evidence of a unified system of self-representations, on the one hand, and the reality of an autonomous structure – the self – on the other.

This confusion results from forgetting that the ego itself makes this reality, by regulating the system of representations. The confusion is perhaps also linked to a conception of the relationship between drive and object that is too naive. When we consider the self as the object of narcissism, do we consider the internal object as having the features of an external one? It is my contention that as there is no external object, the building up of a self-representation results from the creative activity of the ego, but as the fruit of an illusion.

The terms 'object libidinal investment' or 'self libidinal investment' do not imply that we are dealing with an autonomous force – the drive – on the one hand, and with a particular object, on the other. Strictly speaking, we are dealing with the investment of a representation of the object or of the self. It is the mental activity, i.e., the representation, that is invested, and not any internal or external object. A particular activity of the mind presses for actualization and is subsequently actually realized. That is, what we call drive is the pressure for actualization. As soon as a particular 'thought' is realized, its partial discharge stimulates a new activity (displacement, defence, new fantasy, etc.). The terms investment (or cathexis), anticathexis and hypercathexis are related to this activity; and we must be aware that it is by a simplification that we speak of object- or self-investment. In both cases, we really speak of the activity of representation.

In psychoanalytic treatment we investigate the current of representations, and therefore try to evaluate the

dynamic and economic features of this mental activity.
We observe the investment of thoughts but never the
object of the representation. It is clear that we know
nothing about the external object, only something about
its representation. In the same way, do we have to
postulate a hypothetical self in order to study the self-
representations?

A patient, a woman in her thirties, remembers something just at the beginning of the session, early in the
morning: when she was in the underground coming to
my office, she had noticed that the car was full of men.
She and a very young girl were the only women. A fantasy
suddenly springs up in her mind in which the young girl
is assaulted by this group of workers. She was horrified
by this scene, yet now maintains a feeling of disgust and
anger; it is clear that she consciously identifies with the
girl. Next she develops a set of thoughts about the dangers
for a woman in travelling in the underground so early,
and considers the general condition and status of women.
In this way the patient tries to avoid the feelings resulting
from the conscious fantasy. But the conscious fantasy is
related to a latent content.

I notice that she has to use the train so early because I
have fixed the time of the session, and that it is I who
force her to be exposed to those assaults. I notice also
that on some occasions it is clear that during sexual
intercourse she has the fantasy of being raped and that
her pleasure is related to this fantasy. I prefer not to give
any interpretation at this moment. My impression is that
if I interpret my role in the present scene she will agree,
but will have no affective reaction, and use rationalization
or a defence mechanism. If I give an interpretation about
her unconscious rape fantasy, she will deny it because the
self-representation of the independent woman is strongly
invested, and will act as a countercathexis against the
fantasied threat of rape. I do not know if I was right or
wrong in my assumption, but what I want to point out
is that I was coping with two different kinds of self-
representation: the first one conscious (the fantasy in the

train) and preconscious (the necessity of exposing herself to assaults, on account of coming to the session); the second one unconscious (the sexual enjoyment in being raped). A few sessions later, she reported a fantasy she had had while watching a film. As the hero was taking advantage of a naive woman, she became very excited and enjoyed the idea of being such a man. So besides the unconscious fantasy 'of being raped' we may assume that there was the opposite idea, 'of raping'.

It has been emphasized that the self-representation does not achieve a unified structure. Kernberg (1975) described the splitting, in borderline conditions, that affects the self-representation as a whole and the separate sub-structures of representation. Sandler, Holder and Meers (1963) showed the role played by a structure of ideal self-representation as a model for the identity and the integrity of the person. Their concept is very close to that of the ego ideal as it has been described by Nunberg (1932) and Lagache (1961). Since the function of the ego is to build up a coherent image of the self-representation, it must, in solving the neurotic conflict, maintain a compromise between the derivatives of the id and the superego, as is the case for our patient. (In other cases, the construction of a coherent self-representation is a defence against psychotic disintegration.) Before taking into account the superego's demands, however, the ego has to maintain its own unity by preserving a coherent representation of itself. So self-identity is the main goal of the ego's activities, and therefore its representation regulates those activities.

But we must go further. It is still a simplification to speak of object-representation and self-representation. Conscious and unconscious representations are actually made up of scenes that imply a relationship between two protagonists. The patient's fantasies do not really consist of self-representations but of interactions. The conscious fantasy actualizes the scene of a young girl assaulted by men; the preconscious the scene where she is forced, by me, to be exposed to the assaults; the unconscious scenario actualizes the scene where a woman is raped. In the preconscious scene it is easy, too easy, for the patient to identify with the young girl: it is dreadful for a woman to be exposed to such aggression. In the unconscious fantasy, we cannot state that the patient identifies with the subject of the scene. We can reconstruct it in a non-personal way: it is enjoyable for a woman to be raped, to be the passive and masochistic object of a man – but also to be a man behaving in an active and sadistic way.

How can we discriminate between the self- and object-representations? In the unconscious fantasy, the patient may play the role of the passive woman or the role of the active and sadistic man. Thus an unconscious scene which actualizes an interaction between two protagonists has no precise relationship with the self. When we too quickly relate one role to the self and the other to the object, we run the risk of failing to recognize the complexity of the identifications.

Therefore, the task of the ego is to define the identity of the protagonists of the id fantasy and to give a determined role to the self-representation. The ego realizes this personalization in the form of conscious fantasy. It may be argued that we yield to anthropomorphism in attributing to the ego the capacity of judging and choosing among the representations so as to build up a coherent self-representation, or consciousness of oneself, as a spectator identifies himself with one of the protagonists of a scene. So, instead of speaking of the ego as a subject, let us define the ego as all the thoughts that belong together to ensure this identity of the self. We have to consider the dynamic and economic factors that regulate the associative thought processes of the ego's activity. One thought expresses itself as the particular representation of a scene (fantasy, memory or perception). At the same time, according to the rule of the preliminary economic pleasure principle (Widlöcher, 1986), this actualization realizes both a discharge of the investment of that thought and a stimulus to another thought activity. The common denominator of the two thoughts is a component part of the first representation; an aspect of the scene itself; or a characteristic of one of the two protagonists, the subject and the object. When the link depends on the object, it means that an aspect of the object is the common element in two consecutive thoughts. If the same kind of link persists through a longer sequence of representations, this object-representation is consolidated. In economic terms we say that the object-representation is cathected. The self-representation can be cathected in the same way, i.e., as the common element that acts as an axis of the sequence of successive representations.

In our clinical example, it seems clear that the young girl in the underground train, as subject, is linked with a self-representation of the patient's, and that in the hypothetical preconscious associations the self-representation of the patient as subject of the rape is more and more invested. Considering the unconscious and erotic fantasy, however, this process of personalization is not so certain. The unconscious fantasy is centred more *on the action itself* (a woman is being raped or one is raping a woman, as a child is being beaten) than *on the protagonist*. The id fantasy does not engender a self-representation but reinforces the scene itself, leading to a discharge by itself or giving rise to a countercathexis resulting from the ego. In my patient's case I suppose that the preconscious system of self-representation ('What a shame for a woman like me to be exposed to such assaults!') acts as an anticathexis for the unconscious fantasy (of enjoying the rape). So the concept of self-representation as a coherent system results from the dynamic and economic regulations that direct the association of representations, according to the goals of the ego, as support of the feeling of identity and as defence against the id derivatives.

The concept of self results from a double simplification. The self is, as a matter of fact, a set of coherent and permanent self-representations. But the concept of self-representation only defines the axis that regulates all the representations that are centred around the same subject. Finally, the self results from the organization of sets of representations, from a process of investment that rests upon the common denominator of the consecutive thoughts. It is for this reason that we can state that the self results from the ego's activity and characterizes its goal. So the two concepts cannot be separated, and define two characteristics of the same psychic organization.

The next issue I would like to discuss is the origin and development of this structure. Those who consider the ego only as a dynamic regulator of thought activity emphasize its adaptative function and its role in reality-testing. But in pointing out its role in the construction of the self, not only submitted to the reality principle but also subordinated to a principle of coherence, we have to scrutinize how this function is built up. Despite the advantages of using a model of development resulting from early childhood maturation and mother–child relationships, we have to collect clinical data and, in the main, transference processes which may help us, through their pathological expression, to investigate how this function is continuously maintained and reinforced. I assume that this permanent building up results from two processes of identification: one is narcissistic secondary identification, the other the controversial process of primary identification.

The first rests upon the process of introjection. The child internalizes its mother's attitude and develops primary maternal concern in the face of its own psychic reality. Three basic attitudes are introjected: love, security, personalization. By mechanisms of selection and rejection applied to the whole field of mental activity, a self-representation system is built up, that is, an internal representation for the child of a loved self, a secure self, and a personalized self. Anthropomorphism is justified by the fact that the maternal attitude results in the activity of the ego. The child acts upon himself like the mother

144 who loves and protects it. We say that the ego is full of solicitude for its self-representation, the ego-object.

But the child also builds up its own image by another process of identification. The concept of primary identification has undergone many vicissitudes, having been to some extent forgotten and having undergone a splitting process. Little is now made of the parity, postulated by Freud, between object relations and identificatory relations in libidinal development. Rather, the contradictions inherent in his thought have become opposing theoretical systems.

The term primary identification, notwithstanding the multiplicity of descriptions and explanations to which it gives rise, may perhaps best be justified by its instinctual dimension and its establishment of dualism in interaction with the object relation. The wish for identification is primary in that it does not spring from the instincts, as is implied in an object relation. It is perhaps this fact which legitimates its existence as a separate entity, even if, admittedly, this primary wish is exercised in far more complex and varied ways than could at first have been foreseen.

What is the meaning of the wish, in a young child, to identify with another person? A first explanation entails linking it with the 'preliminary stage of object-choice and [the fact] that it is the first way – and one that is expressed in an ambivalent fashion – in which the ego picks out an object' (Freud, 1917, p. 249). In Abraham's descriptions, this stage corresponds to the oral or 'cannibalistic' phase, the fantasy of incorporation of the object being the expression of this first relation to the object. But is it really legitimate to speak of identification? 'Incorporating the object' is in fact an ambiguous phrase. Does it mean incorporation of the object relation – which would correspond to the concept of introjection, but be virtually meaningless from the point of view of the oral object relation? As Green (1973b, p. 150) pointed out, this might make more sense with regard to the avidity with which the hysteric controls the object of his or her sexual wishes. It could also be more appropriate in explaining the ambivalent source of narcissistic identification.

Primary identification would appear, therefore, as the effect of a relation to an 'other' which owes nothing to an object relationship of complementarity. What mode of unconscious representation may answer the wish 'to be the other'? This identification, Freud tells us in *The Ego and the Id* (1923, p. 31), does not seem to be 'the result of the outcome of an object cathexis, it is a direct, immediate and earlier identification than any object cathexis'. Even so, this direct and immediate character does not tell us how the identification is inscribed in psychic reality. If what was involved consisted only in describing the child's behaviour, identification would be reduced to mere imitation. On the other hand, one may content oneself by conceiving of identification as a basic wish, the motive for imitation. But in this case, the term loses all explanatory value. The child imitates because he wishes to identify himself with an 'other'. Yet what is 'a wish to identify oneself with' if there is no representation of this identification as an agent of the wish? We must therefore describe an action which is amenable to being represented, and which may also constitute the matrix of all conscious and unconscious formations – which we will interpret as both the expression and effect of the wish for primary identification. We must then describe a 'scene' which sets up a relation involving the two protagonists of the primary identification, and which is not a comp-lementary object relationship.

Imitation *per se* will not be entirely satisfactory here. In this respect, Gaddini (1969) clearly saw that imitation could not be the behavioural consequence of an uncon-scious fantasy of identification, as Jacobson (1964) supposed. He aimed to reverse the causal chain and saw, in the act of imitation, an initial moment whose internalization in the form of a representation would constitute the unconscious fantasy. Yet how can imitation in the first days of life be described as an action? We say that the infant smiles when the mother smiles or speaks to him. In reality, we are describing two consecutive actions: the mother speaks or smiles, and the infant smiles. Neither of these two actions corresponds to the action of imitating. Now the interest of the concept of projective identification introduced by Klein resides in the way in which it accounts for this interaction in terms of psychic reality. Referring more to its content than to its operational process, Klein's colleague Joan Rivière describes the action as a 'phantasy of forcing the self in part or as a whole into the inside of the object in order to obtain possession and control of it, whether in love or in hate' (in Klein *et al.*, 1952, p. 33). The violent character of this operation may be explained by the role of destructive drives. In this mechanism we find reference to the creation in the 'other' (the object here is external) of a duplicate of the self. The reverse movement, in which the object could be 'reintrojected' in turn, has also been described by Klein. Of course, she conceived of these processes in terms of object relations: what is involved is the control or possession of the object, in Rivière's words, 'through love or hate'; nevertheless, the same movement is clearly involved in both cases: make the other be like oneself, or have oneself made like the other by the other.

As Heimann (1952) underscores, Freud described an identical position with respect to the state of being in love: there the narcissistic over-valuation of the self is projected into the other. The reverse movement, more-over, clearly lies at the origin of the paranoid position, and this relationship between primary identification, transitivism and paranoia was well described by Lacan in 1948 in his paper on aggressivity in psychoanalysis (1966b, p. 113). In what he calls the mirror stage, 'the subject identifies primordially with the visual *Gestalt* of his own body.' In the relationship to the other, a 'normal transitivism' will make him an agent of that which he undergoes, 'the slave identified with the despot, the actor with the spectator, the seduced with the seducer'. To be

the other is to make the other do what one does, or it is to do what the other makes us do. To make the mother smile by smiling or to smile through her smile or speech, in an interaction in which agent and object may hold symmetrical positions, constitutes the matrix on the basis of which representations of identification are possible. To be the other is to make the other be, and to be made by the other. Here we find the mirror relationship no longer conceived of as the mere perception of an image, but as an exercise an imitation. The infant discovers his image in the mirror by making it resemble his action, or by seeking to mimic it. Imitation is not contemplation, but active play as the basis of the transitivism of a relationship of primary identification to the other. In his play with others, the infant practises copying the other and experiences his own power in forcing the other to imitate his own actions.

It may be seen that this relation of reciprocal identification is fundamentally different from an object relationship. The latter is marked by a complementarity of role. The action linking the two protagonists sustains itself, of course, through their difference, but the actions result in institutionalizing this difference, far from eliminating it. On the other hand, in the relationship of primary identification, the intentionality is one of abolishing difference, if the action is based on difference between the protagonists. If, in the object relationship, the action is played out between the two protagonists in the primary relationship of identification, they become confused. The doing is between the one and the other and the two roles are interchangeable.

It seems to me fruitful to consider the construction of the self-object by the ego through this approach of primary identification. To make his own image as a product of the transitive interaction between the ego's primary indentificatory drive and the capacity to realize its own image through a selection of self-representations – this results in the building up of an ideal self: not as an ideal ego, product of the demands of the superego, but as a matrix of uniqueness, of coherence and continuity.

THE DISTINCTION between the ego and the self is, at one and the same time, necessary and relative. It is necessary, to discriminate the regulation of thoughts and actions that characterize the ego and the set of representations that ensure the identity of the person. In the place of Freud's view, in which the ego forces itself upon the id as a love object, we could put the idea that the ego chooses among the id derivatives those that will be built up to create its own love object.

So the self constitutes a stability system that preserves the feeling of identity and uniqueness, while resting upon a narcissistic object relationship. The aim of analysis is to help the ego to ward off the pressures of this model and to assimilate to the self some partial representations that originate from id derivatives. More and more, it is true, we deal with deeply ill patients who do not have a strong and coherent self-image. The psychoanalyst has to take into account the fragility of the self-ego system and to evaluate what amount of partial self-disorganization the patient can tolerate without losing his identity and narcissistic integrity. Obviously, this difficult task has made us more careful about the role of the self as part of the conflict. Rather than an addition to, or a substitute for, ego theory, this care may be seen as a deepening of such theory.

TRANSFERENCE INTERPRETATIONS AND REALITY*

Helmut Thomä

SINCE Strachey's studies (1934, 1937) transference interpretations have been considered the mutative instrument *par excellence*. Since the mutative effect of the transference interpretation, i.e., the change, is tied to the exchange between patient and analyst, Strachey's innovation became the prime example for therapeutically

* This chapter is reprinted from Helmut Thomä and Horst Kächele (1987) *Psychoanalytic Practice*, vol. 1, *Principles*, pp. 277–93. Helmut Thomä writes: 'On the occasion of the first pre-Congress scientific meeting in London in 1961 John Klauber gave a lecture on the structure of the psychoanalytic session. Unknown Germans, amongst them Dr Brigitte Thomä and myself, attended it, and during our postgraduate work in 1962–4 a friendship developed which had a lasting and growing influence on my thinking ... Many of the thoughts expressed in this chapter, and in the textbook *Psychoanalytic Practice*, have their origin in John Klauber's work. He minimized what he called "the split between the analyst's professional and his real personality" (1981, p. 60) in his own career as an analyst, and by describing his personal experience in a very subtle and honest way he promoted this development in others.'

effective exchange processes and for object relationships and their impact on intrapsychic structures.

According to Strachey, in mutative interpretation there is an exchange of superego contents; the attitudes which the analyst communicates by means of his interpretations are internalized by the patient as new and mild parts of the superego. The result of this exchange is thus that the patient partially identifies with the psychoanalyst. Since identification plays such a significant role in therapy, we will discuss it in detail later. Strachey described a type of transference interpretation which alters the patient's experiencing and behaviour. The patient arrives at his new identifications because the analyst assumes the functions of an auxiliary superego.

The concept of mutative interpretation directed attention to exchange processes and thus became the pattern for an interactional understanding of therapy. This evaluation of Strachey's paradigmatic work is the result of independent studies presented by Klauber (1972) and Rosenfeld (1972). Both of these authors emphasize that Strachey's innovation has had a lasting influence on psychoanalytic treatment technique. The contents of mutative transference interpretations have since been substantially extended. Strachey had assumed that especially parts of the superego are projected on to the analyst. Yet the important issue in the theory of projective and introjective identification is no longer the superego, but good and evil parts of the self. Rosenfeld (1972) therefore supplemented the contents of Strachey's mutative interpretation according to the interpretative contents of the Kleinian school.

At the level of the relationship the psychoanalyst functions as more than merely an auxiliary superego, whose stepwise introjection by means of mutative interpretations is, for Strachey, the condition for a cure. Using the terminology of the structural theory of psychoanalysis it is possible to call the psychoanalyst an auxiliary ego. In this function, he helps the patient to gain new insights and thus to interrupt the neurotic repetition compulsion.

Although the analyst contributes to an immediate dissi- pation of anxiety, it would be wrong to equate his function as auxiliary ego with direct support of patients who have weak egos. Strachey limited himself to describing the psychoanalyst's introjection into the patient's superego, but we are today moving toward a two- and three-person psychology as a consequence of the development of psychoanalytic object-relationship psychologies, which assign the patient's identification with the analyst a central position. While it was once possible to assume, in working with a patient displaying superego pathology, that a reliable relationship would develop on its own because the healthy parts of the patient's personality would form a link with the task of analysis despite resistance and repression, in many of today's patients this is no longer possible. It speaks for itself that Kohut (1977) attributes to the analyst the function of a self-object. Here we are dealing with exchange processes in the sense of a primary identification, which creates something shared as the basis for reciprocity and mutuality.

The discovery of the patient's readiness to enter into a therapeutic relationship with the psychoanalyst, to work together to some extent, and to identify with him was paradigmatic. Strachey expressed his surprise

at the relatively small proportion of psychoanalytical literature which has been concerned with the mechanisms by which its therapeutic effects are achieved. A very considerable quantity of data have been accumulated in the course of the last thirty or forty years which throw light upon the nature and workings of the human mind; perceptible progress has been made in the task of classifying and subsuming such data into a body of generalized hypotheses or scientific laws. But there has been a remarkable hesitation in applying these findings in any great detail to the therapeutic process itself. (1934, p. 127, my emphasis)

This observation can be explained by the fact that no specifically psychoanalytic vocabulary was available to describe the curative factors, i.e., those processes that lead *out* of transference neurosis. The description was thus necessarily vague. Some use was made of the terminology of pre-analytic, hypnotic psychotherapy, which was not free of the disrepute attached to suggestive influence. In the model of mutative interpretation, Strachey established a new foundation for the analyst's influence even if it was limited to the exchange of superego contents. Thus is was no longer necessary to borrow elements from pre-analytic theories or from general concepts to explain therapeutic change in certain respects.

How much is still unclear and controversial can be seen from the contradictions in the theories of the therapeutic process and from the difficulties that have been encountered in trying to transform them into practical steps. What does the psychoanalyst contribute towards the creation of a common basis? How does he make it easier for the patient to identify with the joint task and with the analyst, who sheds new light on his problems in coping with life and on his symptoms? An answer to these questions cannot be found by relying on the working relationship in general, but requires that this relationship be translated into individual technical steps. The same is also true for the application of the theory of identification to therapeutic exchange processes. Mutative interpretations are today recognized as belonging to a larger category of interventions. To ease comparison, I would like to refer to two representative passages from a study by Strachey:

It is not difficult to conjecture that these piecemeal introjections of the analyst occur at the moments of the carrying through of transference interpretations. For at those moments, which are unique in the patient's experience, the object of his unconscious impulses simultaneously reveals himself as being clearly aware of their nature, and as feeling on their account neither anxiety nor anger. Thus the object which he introjects at those moments will have a unique quality, which will effectually prevent its undifferentiated absorption into his original superego and will on the contrary imply a step towards a permanent modification in his mental structure. (1937, pp. 144–5)

Strachey then compares the therapeutic effects of the analyst with those of a therapist who employs suggestion:

It is true that the analyst, too, offers himself to his patient as an object and hopes to be introjected by him as a superego. But his one endeavour from the very beginning is to differentiate himself from the patient's archaic objects and to contrive, as far as he possibly can, that the patient shall introject him not as one more archaic imago added to the rest of the primitive superego, but as the nucleus of a separate and new superego . . . He hopes, in short, that he himself will be introjected by the patient as a superego – introjected, however, not at a single gulp *and as an archaic object, whether bad or good, but little by little and* as a real person. (1937, p. 144, my emphasis)

It is improbable that Strachey actually hoped to be consumed as a real person. On the contrary, he probably hoped for a *symbolic internalization*, which coincidentally is said to be characteristic of many cannibalistic rituals (Thomä, 1967, p. 171). In the course of such internalizations both the relation to reality and the self-feeling undergo a change. It is thus possible to say that reality changes as a result of the symbolic interaction.

The current phase of psychoanalytic technique is characterized, according to Klauber (1972, pp. 386–7), by the attempt to distinguish transference from non-transference elements and to describe more precisely the *reality* of the analytic situation. I hope that the discussion in this section will contribute toward this goal.

Klauber gives the following description of the phases since Strachey's unusually influential work. In the *first* phase, attention was directed by what may be the most creative of all the subsequent studies – Alice and Michael Balint's paper 'Transference and countertransference'

(1939) – to the fact that every analyst has an emotional need to do his work in a way which conforms to his personality, and that he thus creates a totally individual and characteristic atmosphere. The question was thus raised whether it were at all possible for the analyst to have a mirror-like attitude, as recommended by Freud. The *second* phase began after World War Two. The therapeutic significance of the analyst's reaction was especially emphasized by Winnicott's study 'Hate in the countertransference' (1949) and by Heimann's paper 'On countertransference' (1950). Central for the *third* phase were the descriptions by Searles (1965) and Racker (1968) of the complex interaction between patient and analyst.

Both mutative interpretations and Strachey's thesis that the analyst in his benign role is introjected into the patient's superego put special emphasis on the problem of reality in the therapeutic situation and on the question of how the analyst's 'real person' has an effect. These issues are as old as psychoanalysis itself. Now, in the midst of the *fourth* phase, it appears to be becoming possible to resolve them technically. We regard the present development as a major step toward integration of the here-and-now and the then-and-there.

We begin by referring to those solutions mentioned by Strachey and emphasized by Klauber, who exhorts us not to over-estimate the content and specificity of interpretations, because they have to be seen in the context of a relationship. The analyst's attitude signalizes, 'I will stay friendly anyway and will not act like the old object; I behave differently than the obsolete anxiety conditions would lead you to expect.' The analyst does not adhere to the principle of an eye for an eye and a tooth for a tooth, thus making it possible to interrupt the vicious circle that Strachey so forcefully described. After all, in the theory of ego development the concept of the superego stands for ways of experiencing and acting that belong to the category of commandments, prohibitions, and ideals. The re-evaluation of these norms is the goal of mutative interpretations according to Strachey. Klauber's argument that this process means the internalization of parts of the psychoanalyst's value system is convincing. A cautious formulation of this view can even be found in some of Strachey's comments.

The real person of the psychoanalyst manifests itself as a 'new object' in the second phase of Strachey's mutative interpretation. In this phase the patient's sense of reality plays a decisive role, and the analyst becomes an archaic transference object during the development of anxiety. The result of the second phase of interpretation depends on the patient's

ability, at the critical moment of the emergence into consciousness of the released quantity of id energy, to distinguish between his phantasy object and the real analyst. The problem here is closely related to one that I have already discussed, namely that of the extreme liability of the analyst's position as auxiliary superego. The analytic situation is all the time threatening to degenerate into a 'real' situation. But this actually means the opposite of what it appears to. It means that the patient is all the time on the brink of turning the real external object (the analyst) into the archaic one; that is to say, he is on the brink of projecting his primitive introjected imagos on to him. In so far as the patient actually does this, the analyst becomes like anyone else that he meets in real life – a phantasy object. The analyst then ceases to possess the peculiar advantages derived from the analytic situation; he will be introjected like all other phantasy objects into the patient's superego, and will no longer be able to function in the peculiar ways which are essential to the effecting of a mutative interpretation. In this difficulty the patient's sense of reality is an essential but a very feeble ally; indeed, an improvement in it is one of the things that we hope the analysis will bring about. It is important, therefore, not to submit it to any unnecessary strain; and that is the fundamental reason why the analyst must avoid any real behaviour that is likely to confirm the patient's view of him as a 'bad' or a 'good' phantasy object. (Strachey, 1934, p. 146)

This hesitation to react, whether in the sense of a good or a bad object, should make it possible for the patient 'to make a comparison between the phantasy external object and the real one' (Strachey, 1934, p. 147). The patient's sense of reality is strengthened as a result of this comparison between the different imagos projected on to the analyst and a more realistic perception. Thus, according to Strachey, there is adjustment to external reality and recognition that the current objects are not good or bad in the archaic sense. Strachey apparently means that differentiated insight relativizes the infantile perceptions, and concludes his argument with the following comment:

It is a paradoxical fact that the best way of ensuring that his ego shall be able to distinguish between phantasy and reality is to withhold reality from him as much as possible. But it is true. His ego is so weak – so much at the mercy of his id and superego – that he can only cope with reality if it is administered in minimal doses. *And these doses are in fact what the analyst gives him, in the form of interpretations.* (Strachey, 1934, p. 147, my emphasis)

The technical problems of Strachey's theses may well be rooted in the contradictions attached to the definition of reality in the analytic situation. Indeed, it is not only in Strachey studies and the discussion of them that this problem is unsolved. The general difficulties result from the fact that

Freud assigns an important part to the notion of reality-testing, *though without ever developing a consistent theoretical explanation of this process and without giving any clear account of its relationship to the reality principle. The way he uses this notion reveals even more clearly that it covers two very different lines of thought: on the one hand, a genetic theory of the learning of reality – of the way in which the instinct is put to the test of*

reality by means of a sort of 'trial-and-error' procedure –
*and, on the other hand, a quasi-transcendental theory
dealing with the constitution of the object in terms of a
whole range of antitheses: internal–external, pleasur-
able–unpleasurable, introjection–projection.* (Laplanche
and Pontalis, 1973, p. 381)

Strachey had apparently thought in terms of antithetical
regulatory principles, i.e., in the framework of the
pleasure and reality principles. Since, according to theory,
the pleasure principle is merely modified by the reality
principle, the search for gratification on a real (material)
object remains the determining factor. On the other hand,
psychic reality is moulded by unconscious wishes and
fantasies. Freud believed it necessary to assume a contradiction between these realities, because the incest taboo
and other inevitable frustrations limit material gratification while at the same time constituting the actually
desired reality:

*It was only the non-occurrence of the expected satisfac-
tion, the disappointment experienced, that led to the
abandonment of this attempt at satisfaction by means of
hallucination. Instead of it, the psychical apparatus had
to decide to form a conception of the* real circumstances
in the external world and to endeavour to make a real
alteration in them. A new principle of mental functioning
was thus introduced; *what was presented in the mind was
no longer what was agreeable but what was real, even if
it happened to be disagreeable.* (Freud 1911, p. 219, my
emphasis)

Assuming that the object relationships are regulated by
the pleasure and reality principles, then the experienced
reality is determined by the dominance of the one or other
principle. It is characteristic of psychoanalytic theory to
view the pleasure principle as the primary and archaic
fact, which is inexhaustible and derives from the unconscious, the id. It certainly makes a big difference whether
I only imagine something or whether I can actually

grasp an object or in some way immediately perceive it (Hurvich, 1970; Kafka, 1977). Yet this is not a contradiction between different realities, which would have to be taken into consideration and would inevitably lead to the irresolvable problem of 'why the child should ever have to seek a real object if it can attain satisfaction on demand, as it were, by means of hallucination' (Laplanche and Pontalis, 1973, p. 381). Since transference interpretations also involve the analyst as an individual, we have to add a few more comments on psychic reality. Referring to the *real* person of the analyst precipitates concerns, as if psychic levels were supposed to be sacrificed and replaced by materialization, i.e., wish-fulfilment.

Reflection on the theory of psychic reality is necessary. Like McLaughlin (1981), we believe that we can come closer to a solution to these problems by viewing the analytic meeting from the perspective of *psychic reality*, i.e., as a *scheme* which is both comprehensive and contains different meanings. Patient and analyst naturally experience the situation very concretely, with their subjective wishes, affects, expectations, hopes, and ways of thinking. As soon as we reflect on our different psychic states, a plan develops for ordering our experiences and events with regard to space and time. To a great extent a person follows his subjective schemata for thinking and acting, which thus govern his behaviour, without reflecting on them. He experiences the fact that psychic reality is constituted situationally in interpersonal relations. Psychic reality in McLaughlin's sense refers both to concrete subjective experiences and to their unconscious roots. The analyst constructs a patient's psychic reality within the framework of the psychoanalytic theory he uses. Such constructions are aids to orientation.

McLaughlin also includes the analyst's countertransference in his comprehensive understanding. The many levels of meaning of the concrete psychic realities, including the underlying theories held by both the patient and analyst, are interrelated and understood interactionally. The security which the analyst could have drawn from the mirror analogy is thus lost. McLaughlin shows that reflection on psychic reality is very productive, even though the analyst may initially have to put up with insecurity since, according to McLaughlin, he can no longer proceed from an understanding of himself as a real person who enters into a realistic relationship with the patient. Everything is relativized by the patient's perspective. Reality develops in this two-person relationship by means of an interactive process in which the participants' subjective perspectives are continually tested and a certain consensus is reached. Patient and analyst learn to make themselves understood. The result of a successful analysis is a gradual and mutual confirmation of the psychic realities and their authentication, a term McLaughlin uses to describe a process of change. In this way both participants acquire *relative* security with regard to their perspectives.

The analyst is affected by the critical discussion that takes place in the psychoanalytic dialogue. He is the expert, not only employing common sense but also expressing opinions that he has acquired during his training. His professionalism has moulded his thinking. His view of a patient's psychic reality (as well as his experience of his own) is not independent of the theories that he uses. In testing authentication we have to go further than McLaughlin and raise the question of whether the indirect source of some of the problems we face should not be sought in Freud's theories on psychic reality.

We are dealing with a region of high tension between poles marked by the antithetical concepts of psychic reality vs. material reality, reality principle vs. pleasure principle, pleasure-ego vs. reality-ego. Ultimately we arrive at reality-testing as the act that distinguishes between internal and external, or between what is merely imagined and what is actually perceived. Freud opposed psychic reality to material reality after he was forced to give up his theories of seduction and of the pathogenic role of real infantile traumata. Fantasies not derived from real events possess the same pathogenic value for the subject which Freud originally attributed to unconscious memories of actual events. The contrast between the two realities is thus linked to contents characterizing the realities. Psychic reality is the world of the subjective, conscious, and unconscious wishes and fantasies, and material reality is characterized by the actual gratification or non-gratification of instinctual needs on objects.

According to Laplanche and Pontalis (1973, p. 363) psychic reality designates 'unconscious desire and its associated fantasies'. Is it necessary to attribute reality to unconscious desires? Freud asks this question in the context of dream analysis, answering:

If we look at unconscious wishes reduced to their most fundamental and truest shape, we shall have to conclude, no doubt, that psychical *reality is a particular form of existence not to be confused with* material *reality.* (1900, p. 620)

Thus there is both psychic reality and material reality. The decisive sentence with regard to the psychoanalytic view of the genesis and nature of neuroses reads: 'The phantasies possess *psychical* as contrasted with *material* reality, and we gradually learn to understand that *in the world of the neuroses it is psychical reality which is the decisive kind*' (Freud, 1916–17, p. 368).

In Freud's theory, psychic reality is regulated by the pleasure principle, which itself is moulded in human development by life's necessities by means of the reality principle. Reality-testing is subordinate to the reality principle. The growing child learns to postpone immediate gratification in order to find a more realistic gratification of its needs, i.e., one based on mutuality and congruence with the needs of fellow man. The tension between psychic and material realities is thus based on the assumption that there is a surplus of desires continually seeking gratification but not finding it because of life's necessities in general and the incest taboo in particular. To create more favourable conditions a certain amount of gratification in the therapuetic situation is necessary; otherwise the old frustations would simply be repeated. The problem of frustration and gratification in the analytic situation becomes easier to solve if the theory of psychic reality is deepened and not linked with *frustration* in a one-sided fashion. In fact, it is necessary and essential therapeutically that the patient be enabled to reach many joyful congruences with the object, i.e., the analyst, and to discuss differences of opinion. This facilitates the path to the frustrated unconscious childhood desires seeking gratification in the present.

The purpose of these comments is to indicate the consequences of a comprehensive conception of psychic reality. The patient seeks and hopes for an improvement or cure of his symptoms and difficulties, that is, he hopes to achieve a positive change with the help of an expert. His attempt to relate all of his feelings and thoughts reveals a multi-faceted image of the world in which he lives. He describes different views of his world depending on his mood and on the predominance of different desires, expectations, hopes, and anxieties. Although the patient also distinguishes between his perceptions of people and things and his ideas about them, he does not divide reality into a psychic sphere and a material one. This is true despite his awareness that his desires and ideas may conflict, and that he is dependent on external objects in his search for pleasure and gratification. Very diverse processes take place in the analyst when he listens and lets his emotions and thoughts reach a conclusion. If the analyst intervenes at any point with a comment, the patient is confronted with information. Yet, as Watzlawick *et al.* (1967) say, it is impossible not to communicate, since negative information, e.g., the analyst's silence, also constitutes a communication, particularly when the patient expects some kind of response.

The psychoanalyst's comments introduce points of view that the patient must confront in some manner – he can ignore them, accept them, reject them, etc. Sooner or later there will be joint reflection on various issues. Present during this reflection, either consciously or unconsciously, are many third parties: family members, other relatives, and people the patient knows, works with, and lives with. The analyst's own experiences, desires, longings, old anxieties, and current struggles are constantly touched on. Since he himself is not the one who is suffering, he can for the good of the patient find a distance from which he can presume the existence of a wish when the patient momentarily reacts with anxiety. The emotional and intellectual burdens of this activity on the analyst would of course be too great to bear if he did not have a wealth of explanatory sketches at his disposal which reflect typical conflict patterns. They facilitate his orientation during therapy.

Relating these points to Strachey's understanding of reality, we find the following. In his statement that 'the analytic situation is all the time threatening to degenerate into a "real" situation', Strachey refers to the pleasure principle in a wide sense of the term (1934, p. 146). He starts from introjected imagos that are then projected on to the analyst without taking situational precipitating factors into consideration. Noteworthy is that Strachey assumes fixed quantities both here and when speaking of the real, external object, i.e., the psychoanalyst. It is clear from the passage quoted above that Strachey believed it possible to use *withdrawal of reality* to reinforce the patient's capacity for differentiation when *testing reality* at the time of the mutative transference interpretation.

By following the mirror analogy, the analyst may get involved in a role conflict which keeps him from confirming the patient's rather realistic perceptions in transference interpretations and thus prevents him from working against new denials and repressions. Heimann (1956) did not notice, despite her early innovative contribution on countertransference (1950), that it is impossible to be, on the one hand, a mirror having no self and no independent existence, but only reflecting the patient; and, on the other, a person who is part of the analytic situation and of the patient's problems both at a realistic level and at a fantasy one. It suffices if the analyst demonstrates some restraint, enabling the patient to re-enact in transference the relationship patterns which have remained active unconsciously.

In the context of the extension of the theory of transference (in the sense of a comprehensive concept of transference) our considerations have to lead to the view that the analyst's so-called reality is constituted during the patient's constant unconscious and conscious testing. In the instant he makes a mutative interpretation, the analyst also reveals something of himself, as Strachey emphasizes. This certainly does not refer to just any personal confession. What is directly or indirectly expressed in helpful interpretations is enriched by the analyst's professionalism and by the fact that his experience is independent of an overly narrow subjectivity. The analyst's professional knowledge facilitates a cognitive process which opens up new avenues for the patient to find solutions. These are by no means personal confessions, but communications – whether non-verbal or in the form of interpretations – about how the analyst views a patient's problem, how he himself feels and thinks in this regard, and what and how he is in regard to the patient. In this sense I agree with Rosenfeld (1972, p. 458) that the psychoanalyst's interpretations may reflect very clearly what he is.

Especially important in this regard is the *spontaneity* of the analyst, as Klauber emphasizes:

Various technical consequences follow from this emphasis on spontaneity. Spontaneous exchanges humanize the analytical relationship by the continual interchange of partial identifications. It is this human quality of the relationship which is the antidote to the traumatic quality of transference as much or more than the acceptance of impulses by an analyst who reinforces the benign qualities of the superego. (1981, p. 116)

The precondition for this cognitive process which includes the other ego, the analyst, is of course that the analyst does not withdraw by proffering purely reductive transference interpretations. Gill's (1982) systematic analysis of the factors precipitating transference and, especially, resistance to transference following very plausible preconscious perceptions makes it possible to provide an answer to the question of what the analyst is as a real person in the therapeutic situation. The here-and-now must be considered in its interrelationship with the then-and-there, and in the process new and innovative perspectives are opened. Freud (1933, p. 74) contrasted the immutability of the repressed, the so-called timelessness of the unconscious, to analytic work, which overcomes the power of the past. The here-and-now is linked with the then-and-there in the process in which something becomes conscious, and precisely this is the mutative effect of transference interpretations.

The analyst must be patient, because it takes some time before unconscious processes manifest themselves in transference in such a way that therapeutically effective interpretations are possible. This is what is meant by Freud's statement that from 'the physician's point of view I can only declare that in a case of this kind he must behave as "timelessly" as the unconscious itself, if he wishes to learn anything or to achieve anything' (1918, p. 10). Note that 'timelessly' is in quotation marks; from the context it is clear that transferences also develop in severe cases if the analyst waits patiently. *Once* the timelessness of the unconscious has been overcome, it even becomes possible significantly to reduce the length of treatment for such severe illnesses, according to Freud, because it enables the analyst with increasing experience to make helpful transference interpretations, i.e., those linking the past with the present. The repetitions create the impression that time is standing still. The dreaming ego also has time feeling and is aware of objections (Freud, 1900, p. 326; Hartocollis, 1980). It is therefore misleading to speak of the timelessness of the unconscious when referring to the time feeling at different levels of consciousness.

My line of argument is important for understanding 165 the mutative effect of transference interpretations because they link past and present. In Freud's view, past, unconsciously preserved wishes lose their effect when they reach consciousness. This leads to the conclusion that transference interpretations which assume that the patient's perceptions and experiences in the here-and-now are ahistorical repetitions miss the point just as much as interpretations of the here-and-now which ignore the unconscious dimension of the individual's life.

The emphasis on the ahistorical quality of unconscious processes and their interpretation in the here-and-now often goes together with a very strict application of the mirroring function. Ezriel's (1963) studies start from the assumption that the ahistorical re-enactment in transference is more complete the more passive and abstinent the well-analysed analyst is. Such an analyst directs his interpretations at the object relationships which are unconsciously sought or avoided. Ezriel recommends a type of transference interpretation oriented on the object relationship which is sought but anxiously avoided. For this reason his interpretations always contain an explanatory 'because', as in the sentence, 'You are now avoiding this wish to relate that fantasy *because* you fear rejection.'

Close examination of Ezriel's work leads to the realization that his description of the psychoanalytic method as ahistorical is not justified. It is true that the therapeutic effectiveness of the psychoanalytic method is related to the here-and-now and to the knowledge that can be acquired in the analytic situation. Yet Ezriel's conception is based on the assumption that the unconscious is ahistorical. Thus the patient's present realistic perceptions also do not play an indeper lent role even though only here-and-now interpretation are given; such interpretations refer exclusively to seemingly ahistorical, momentarily effective, unconscious forces and constellations. Mutative qualities could not be in the here-and-now if the unconscious constellations were timeless, excluded from the individual's past, and ahistorical. We have highlighted

Ezriel's work here because he assigned the here-and-now a special methodological significance; however, his studies failed because, among other factors, he neglected to give the analyst's situational influence the same importance in practice as he did in theory.

The inclusion of personal influence and realistic perceptions in transference interpretations is the central issue distinguishing Freud's reconstructive genetic transference interpretations from the innovations which followed upon Strachey's publications. If the corrective object relationship in the analytic situation is referred to, as Segal (1973, p. 123) does, then the analyst is bound to include the influencing subject (the analyst) and the patient's realistic perceptions of the analyst in the formulation of transference interpretations. The importance of psychic reality and unconscious fantasies is by no means diminished by the discovery that realistic observations, for example the analyst's countertransference, play a role in their genesis.

The patient participates in the psychoanalyst's value system whenever it is of consequence for new solutions to neurotic conflicts. This identificatory participation, which Strachey described in his re-evaluation of the superego, commandments, and proscriptions, is not only inevitable, it is therapeutically necessary. Trying to avoid it leads to a strained atmosphere which may be characterized by anxious avoidance of therapeutically necessary participation.

The findings of research in the social sciences make it essential that great importance be attached to the psychoanalyst's influence on the situational origin of perceptions and fantasies. The theories about the handling of real relationships also affect the structuring of the therapeutic situation. Since in Freud's theory the reality principle is secondary to the pleasure principle and real gratification is always sought – even though gratification may be delayed for varying periods of time – tension develops in the therapy as a result of frustration and renunciation. Creating an atmosphere of this kind can

provide relief to a group of inhibited patients because
only empathy and tolerance toward the aggressions produced by frustration can lead to some alleviation of the
superego. The transformation of an excessively strict
superego into a mild one does not create the kind of
therapeutic problems that have to be solved in the repair of
defective ego functions or the construction of previously
underdeveloped ones. The patient's identification with
the psychoanalyst plays a decisive role in this. It seems as
if this category of patients is increasing in number, and it
is therefore important to determine the conditions under
which identifications are formed.

The relationship of transference interpretations to the
other aspects of the therapeutic relationship received too
little attention in the one-sided reception of Strachey's
position. Klauber's (1972) work is the most outstanding
of the few exceptions. Strachey had ascribed to these
other components, such as suggestion, lessening anxiety,
and abreacting, an important role in treatment. However,
the problem of how the analyst presents his real self to
the patient in small doses has not been solved.

As in the discussion between Greenson, Heimann, and
Wexler (1970), controversies continue as to how the
analyst should handle realistic perceptions in the here-
and-now. Some analysts fear that this could ultimately
lead to the gratification of needs and mean that treatment
would no longer be conducted in a state of *frustration*
and *abstinence*. These problems of technique can be
solved constructively and to the advantage of therapeutic
change if we understand their origin in the psychoanalytic
theory of reality. In discussing this point we will start
from the following observation by Adorno:

*On the one hand, 'libido' is for it [psychoanalysis] the
actual psychic reality: gratification is positive, frustration
negative because it leads to illness. On the other hand,
psychoanalysis accepts the civilization which demands
the frustration, if not completely uncritically, then at least
in resignation. In the name of the reality principle it*

justifies the individual psychic sacrifice without subjecting the reality principle itself to rational scrutiny. (Adorno, 1952, p. 17)

Although the reality principle that the analyst represents is relatively mild, it should cause enough frustration 'to bring this conflict to a head, to develop it to its highest pitch, in order to increase the instinctual force available for its solution' (Freud 1937a, p. 231). This statement from one of Freud's later texts shows that technical problems result from the psychoanalytic theory of reality.

Subjecting the reality principle to rational scrutiny can only mean, with regard to technique, that the patient's perceptions must be taken seriously. In the moment that this takes place, an intentional act finds its object, thus creating reality. We will return to this topic later when discussing the relationship between historical truth and perception in the here-and-now. Since the individual's conception of reality is determined in a socio-cultural context, neither the one nor the other can be taken as absolute. The reality of the psychoanalytic situation is thus constituted in the exchange, assimilation, and rejection of opinions.

Neither the analyst nor the patient starts from a completely valid standpoint when testing reality. In the one case we would end up adjusting to the existing conditions, in the other in solipsism. At the one extreme the individual declares that his family or society is insane and the cause of his illness, at the other the individual is dependent on and made ill by external factors. Carrying this polarization to its limits, society as a whole could be declared insane and the emotionally disturbed could be considered to be the healthy individual revolting against sick society. Successful therapy would then adjust this person to the sick society without noticing it. Adorno goes this far when he writes, 'By becoming similar to the insane totality, the individual becomes truly sick' (1955, p. 57).

ILLUSION AND
SPONTANEITY IN
PSYCHOANALYSIS

A mutative interpretation seems to have a special effect

if it is devised to strengthen the working relationship, i.e., the patient's *identification* with the psychoanalyst in his role as *auxiliary ego*. As a result of the great influence exerted by Strachey's work a new form of 'interpretation fanaticism' developed. This had been previously criticized by Ferenczi and Rank (1924), on the grounds that it referred to genetic reconstructions which neglect experience in the here-and-now and are thus therapeutically ineffective. Strachey (1934, p. 158) also examined this unsuccessful interpretation fanaticism and pointed to the emotional immediacy inherent in his mutative interpretation (as transference interpretation) at the decisive moment of urgency. At the same time he emphasized that the majority of interpretations do not refer to transference.

Nevertheless, a new form of interpretation fanaticism developed, this time with reference to 'transference' in the sense of pure repetition. This limited the therapeutic effectiveness of psychoanalysis for a different reason than excessive intellectual reconstruction did. The consequence of understanding everything that occurs in the analytic situation, or is mentioned by the patient, primarily as a manifestation of transference is, as Michael Balint (1968, p. 169) emphasized, that 'the principal frame of reference used for formulating practically every interpretation is a relationship between a highly important, omnipresent object, the analyst, and an unequal subject who at present apparently cannot feel, think, or experience anything unrelated to his analyst'.

The inequality which develops can lead to malignant regressions if the external circumstances of a patient's life are neglected in favour of ahistorical transference interpretations. Such interpretations refer to those interpretations which exclude the present in all its forms – the analytic situation, the analyst's influence, and external circumstances. If the present is viewed solely as repetition of the past or of unconscious schemata derived from the past, which Freud described as templates or clichés, transference interpretations do not refer to a

170 genuine situation which has a basis in the present reality. Strictly speaking, the here-and-now is then nothing more than a new imprint of an old pattern or template.

In contrast to the ahistorical conception of transference and the interpretations associated with this view, authentic interpretations of the here-and-now provide new experiences because they take the present seriously. Here the psychoanalyst fulfils a genuine task that cannot be reduced to that of father or mother. Heimann (1978) used the expression 'supplementary ego' to describe this function, traced it back to the mother, and also called it the 'maternal function'. Because of the danger of a reductionist misunderstanding, we do not want to call the therapeutic supplementary or auxiliary ego maternal, but only to adopt the designation of the *function*, which is the essential aspect.

The mother [in the person of the analyst], as supplementary ego, offers the child [the patient] concepts that it does not have itself. The mother teaches the child new concepts of thinking and thus sets it on the path of progress. (Heimann, 1978, p. 228)

Freud's technical demand that 'the patient should be educated to liberate and fulfil his own nature, not to resemble ourselves' seems to contradict the great therapeutic significance of the patient's identification with the analyst (Freud, 1919, p. 165). Another passage (Freud, 1940, p. 181) reads, 'We serve the patient in various functions, as an authority and a substitute for his parents, as a teacher and educator.' On the other hand, Freud warns:

However much the analyst may be tempted to become a teacher, model and ideal for other people and to create men in his own image, he should not forget that that is not his task in the analytic relationship, and indeed that he will be disloyal to his task if he allows himself to be led on by his inclinations. (1940, p. 175)

At a symposium on the termination of treatment, Hoffer

(1950) described the patient's capacity to identify with the psychoanalyst's functions as the most important component of the therapeutic process and its success. This topic thus has fundamental significance for understanding the therapeutic process, if for no other reason than that it closely associates the psychoanalyst's *functions* with the patient's *identifications*.

Consideration must be given to a whole series of theoretical and practical problems which I would now like to outline by formulating a few questions. What does the patient identify with? What are the consequences of the psychoanalytic theory of identification for the optimization of practice, with the goal of making it easier for the patient to assimilate the functions mediated by the analyst? What does the psychoanalyst mediate, and how does he do it? With regard to the patient's experience, is it possible to distinguish the functions from the person who has them? How does the psychoanalyst indicate that he is fundamentally different from the expectations which characterize transference neuroses and the consequences they have on the processes of perception? Does it suffice for the patient to recognize that the way the psychoanalyst thinks and acts does not conform to the established patterns of expectations? Does it suffice for the analyst to define himself negatively, i.e., by not conforming to the patient's unconscious expectations? In our opinion, such a lack of conformity does not suffice to interrupt neurotic repetition compulsion and the therapeutic function is rooted in the fact that the psychoanalyst works in an innovative manner, introducing new points of view and enabling the patient to find previously unattainable solutions to problems.

The innovative elements occupy such a natural role in therapy that they have, almost unnoticed, become part of the point of view that a *synthesis* takes place apparently on its own. Yet the psychoanalyst's interventions in fact contain at least latent goals which help to determine how the released elements are reassembled. The fundamental therapeutic function of the psychoanalyst is that he is

172   effective as a 'substitute'. Regardless of whether he is
viewed as an auxiliary superego or an auxiliary ego, and
however the current school-determined language of
theory and practice deviates from Strachey's, it is a generally accepted psychoanalytic experience that support
initiates the exchange processes which lead to new identifications. The result is a lack of independence on the part
of the patient, leading among other things to the necessity
that he speak his therapist's language, as Michael Balint
(1968, p. 93) described the situation, showing great
understanding of this connection between language,
thinking, and acting.

Learning from a model – or, in psychoanalytic terminology, identification – has a significance in every therapeutic process which can hardly be exaggerated. Since the
very different object relationship theories of the various
psychoanalytic schools become a focus of attention,
all concepts referring to the relationship of internal to
external and of subject to subject (or object) are of special
technical interest (Kernberg, 1979; Meissner, 1979;
Ticho, according to Richards, 1980). In his introduction
to a conference on object relationship theory, Kanzer
(1979, p. 315) calls special attention to the fact that the
emphasis given to object relationships has made it possible
to develop a dyadic understanding of the traditional
treatment of adults. He also refers to numerous authors
who have furthered this development (Michael Balint,
1950; Spitz, 1956; Loewald, 1960; Stone, 1961;
Gitelson, 1962).

Common to internalization, identification, introjection, and incorporation is that they all refer to a movement
from without to within, involving assimilation, appropri-
ation, and adaptation (Schafer, 1968; Meissner, 1979;
McDevitt, 1979). Regardless of the meaning attached to
these words – e.g., incorporation taken literally and too
concretely, identification as symbolic equating – their
common feature is that they refer to an object relationship. Michael Balint (1968, pp. 61–2) therefore pointed
out that it is not possible to talk about identifications in

a narrow sense of the word unless there is a certain
distance between within and without or between subject
and object. Freud's fundamental anthropological observation deserves to be mentioned in this connection; he
noted that relinquished object relationships are expressed
in identifications (1923, p. 29). It hardly needs to be
emphasized how significant this aspect of identification
is in separation, bereavement, and the termination of
analyses.

We believe that it is now possible to solve the old
problem concerning reality in the psychoanalytic situation, and that fifty years after Strachey's important
article psychoanalytic technique can and will consider-
ably expand its therapeutic potential. Transference
interpretations play a special role in this development. In
our argument we have so far distinguished the following
aspects:

1. Here-and-now interpretations can be taken to
include every kind of reference to the analytic situation,
but not to the patient's current circumstances outside of
analysis or to those prior to analysis. An extension of the
concept of transference creates two classes of inter-
vention: one relates to everything that is outside the
analytic situation, the other includes all interpretations
concerning the here-and-now in the comprehensive
understanding of transference. In the traditional form of
transference interpretation, the analyst assumes there is
a *repetition* and thus focuses his attention on the *genesis*.
These statements are based on the assumption that there
is a conditional relationship between current experiencing
and behaviour and earlier experiences. In other words,
such transference interpretations read something like
'You are anxious because you are afraid that I will punish
you just like your father did.'

2. It is possible for transference interpretations to
be directed more towards the genesis and towards the
reconstruction of memories. In contrast, it is also possible
for the here-and-now to move to the centre of the
interpretation if *unconscious processes* are assumed to be

174   *ahistorical*. Of course, the subject matter of this kind of
transference interpretation is the analyst as an *old* object.
Furthermore, the momentary dynamic is nearly identical
to the conserved (ahistorical) genesis. In the here-and-
now interpretations, the differences between the material
which has been transformed from the past into the present
and the analyst's contribution to transference are levelled
out. There is no investigation of the affective and cognitive
processes creating the momentary psychic reality. The
purpose of the analyst's mirror-like attitude is to manifest
the ahistorical unconscious fantasies and the unconscious
defence processes directed against them in the purest
form.

3. We come finally to the type of transference interpretations in the here-and-now which realize both the potential for dyadic knowledge provided by the psychoanalytic
method *and* its therapeutic effectiveness. We are thinking
of all those transference interpretations which consider
in a comprehensive manner the impact of the patient's
more or less realistic perceptions on the unconscious
processes. In this context we can refer to Klauber's
conception that one task of psychoanalysis in the current
phase is to distinguish the transference from the non-
transference elements in the psychoanalytic situation.
In the meantime, however, transference theory has
expanded so much that speaking of non-transference
elements creates misunderstandings. Of course, it is essential to distinguish between the imaginative decorations
and the wishful image of the world facilitated in the
analytic situation, on the one hand, and the realistic
elements of the analyst's behaviour, on the other. This
process of differentiating the kinds of dyadic knowledge
constitutes the mutative effect of transference
interpretations.

We can now mention Arlow's (1979) view that transference develops by means of metaphoric thinking. On
the basis of unconscious schemata (Freud's templates),
psychic reality is formed from the points of view of

ILLUSION AND
SPONTANEITY IN
PSYCHOANALYSIS

contrast and similarity. The patient compares the psycho- analytic situation and the psychoanalyst with current and previous experiences. If transference is viewed as a manifestation of metaphoric thinking and experience, as Arlow views it, it is necessary to assume that the *similarity* makes it possible to establish a connection, to carry something from one shore to the other, i.e., from a previous to the current situation. Precisely from the therapeutic points of view, therefore, Carveth's (1984, p. 506) criticism must be taken seriously. He points out that the analyst's *confirmation* of the similarity is *the* precondition for changing the transference templates, which according to psychoanalytic theory have been formed by the necessity of denying realistic perceptions and of repressing affective and cognitive processes. Freud's unconscious templates are very similar to the linguistic category of 'dead metaphors' (Weinrich, 1968; Carveth, 1984). These can come to life, i.e., manifest themselves out of the dynamic unconscious, if similarities (in the sense meant by Gill) are admitted and acknowledged in transference interpretations. Otherwise there is a repetition of acts of denial, and the old templates maintain their influence. The moment that similarities are identified also marks the discovery of the here-and-now and the then-and-there. The differentiation of kinds of dyadic knowledge makes it possible for the mutative interpretation to exert a corrective emotional experience.

Finally, we would like to point out that our view draws its therapeutic application from Freud's fundamental assertion that 'a fragment of *historical truth*' is contained in all emotional disturbances (1937b, p. 269). Freud emphasizes that if this historical truth were acknowledged, then:

The vain effort would be abandoned of convincing the patient of the error of his delusion and of its contradiction of reality; and, on the contrary, the recognition of its kernel of truth would afford common ground upon which the therapeutic work could develop. That work would

176 *consist in liberating the fragment of historical truth from its distortions and its attachments to the actual present day and in leading it back to the point in the past to which it belongs. The transposing of material from a forgotten past on to the present or on to an expectation of the future is indeed a habitual occurrence in neurotics no less than in psychotics.* (1937b, pp. 267–8)

It should be clear how we would like to make this conception therapeutically useful. The common ground can be found in the *recognition of the kernel of truth* in transference interpretations. In doing this, it is as a rule sufficient to acknowledge the general human disposition. Constructions of historical truths are, in contrast, dubious; they lack the power of conviction emanating from current experience. We believe that the patient, in comparing the here-and-now and the then-and-there, ultimately establishes a distance to each, freeing himself for the future. We would therefore like to paraphrase a statement of Freud's (1937a, pp. 231–2) to the effect that the analytic work proceeds best when the patient establishes distance between himself and both past experiences and current truths, which then become history.

JOHN KLAUBER was born in London in 1917. He graduated in modern history from Christ Church College, Oxford. During the war he served in the army as a Captain in the Intelligence Corps. He qualified as a doctor in 1951, and became a Member of the British Psycho-Analytical Society in 1953. Within the Society he served in turn as Honorary Business Secretary, Honorary Scientific Secretary, and Chairman of the Scientific Committee from 1971 to 1976. He was also Chairman of the Medical Section of the British Psychological Society in 1967, becoming a Fellow of the BPS in 1971. In 1972 he was Foundation Fellow of the Royal College of Psychiatrists.

John Klauber was Honorary Consultant Psychoanalyst at the London Clinic of Psycho-Analysis from 1959 to 1968. From the early 1960s he helped re-establish psychoanalysis in Germany, paying frequent visits to several German psychoanalytic societies to lecture and lead seminars. During this period he was also Psychotherapist in the newly founded Academic Department of Psychiatry at the Middlesex Hospital Medical School. In 1980 and until his death in August 1981 he was President of the British Psycho-Analytical Society. His last appointment was as Freud Memorial Visiting Professor at

University College London; he died shortly before delivering these lectures.

NICOLE BERRY practises psychoanalysis in a town situated half way between Paris and London. As an analyst she was attached to a paediatric unit in Rouen hospitals and then taught at the University of Rouen for some years; she now works exclusively with adults. She is a Member of the French Psycho-analytic Association, and regularly leads seminars for analysts in training.

At a very early stage in her career, she felt an affinity with English psychoanalysts, and her thought is closely related to that of Winnicott and Fairbairn. She is a contributor to the *Nouvelle Revue de Psychanalyse* and has also published in the *Revue Française de Psychanalyse*. She recently completed a book on the feeling of identity, *Le Sentiment d'identité* (Paris: Editions Universitaires, forthcoming), and is currently interested in the application of psychoanalysis to literary studies, in particular to the work of Thomas Mann, Henry James (Berry, 1983) and the Austrian writer Alfred Kubin.

PATRICK CASEMENT was originally a social worker, having studied anthropology and theology at Cambridge. He subsequently trained with the British Association of Psycho-therapists and started in full-time private practice in 1973. He qualified as a psychoanalyst in 1977 and became a training analyst of the British Psycho-Analytical Society in 1984. He is the author of *On Learning from the Patient* (Tavistock Publications, 1985) and has published a number of papers on issues related to technique in psychotherapy and psycho-analysis.

ROGER KENNEDY was originally trained as a physiologist, physician and child psychiatrist. He now works as a Consultant Psychotherapist with families at the Cassel Hospital and with adolescents at the Brent Consultation Centre, both in London. He is also an Associate Member of the British Psycho-Analytical Society and a psychoanalyst in private practice. He is co-author of *The Works of Jacques Lacan: An Introduction* (Free Association Books, 1986), and co-editor of *The Family as In-Patient: Families and Adolescents at the Cassel Hospital* (Free Association Books, 1987).

NEVILLE SYMINGTON is a Member of the British Psycho-
Analytical Society, and was a member of the Scientific
Committee and the Committee for the Application of Psycho-
Analysis at the Institute of Psycho-Analysis, London. For
several years he worked in the Adult Department at the Tavistock Clinic, London where, together with others, he was
responsible for supervising and tutoring on the Clinic's four-
year training in psychotherapy. He also pioneered a workshop
on psychotherapy with the mentally handicapped, which was
a special interest. His lectures on psychoanalytic theory are
now published as *The Analytic Experience: Lectures from the
Tavistock* (Free Association Books, 1986).

In 1986 Neville Symington moved to Sydney, where he is in
private practice together with his wife, who is also a psychoanalyst. At conferences in Australia and New Zealand he has
given papers on 'The possibility of human freedom and its
transmission' and 'The analyst's inner task'; he is also doing
research on psychoanalysis, evolution and religion.

HELMUT THOMÄ has been Chairman of the Department of
Psychotherapy of the University of Ulm and Director of the
Psychoanalytic Institute in Ulm since 1967. A representative
of the first postwar generation of German analysts, he did
advanced work at the Psychosomatic Hospital of the University
of Heidelberg under Alexander Mitscherlich, at the Yale Psychi-
atric Institute, and at the Institute of Psycho-Analysis in
London. He is the author of numerous articles in both English
and German; his book *Anorexia Nervosa* (New York: International Universities Press, 1967) was one of the first postwar
psychoanalytic studies to be translated into English. Thomä
was President of the German Psychoanalytical Association
from 1968 to 1972.

DANIEL WIDLÖCHER is Professor of Psychiatry and Chief
Physician in the Department of Psychiatry at the Salpêtrière
Hospital in Paris. A Member of the French Psychoanalytic
Association, he has been Secretary of the International Psycho-
analytical Association and President of the European Feder-
ation for Psychoanalysis. His current work is centred on
depression, and he is the author of *Les Logiques de la dépression*
(Paris: Fayard, 1984). Equally concerned with a revision of
psychoanalytic metapsychology, he recently published *Méta-*
psychologie du sens (Paris: Presses Universitaires de France,

180   1986). In 1979 he co-edited, with Edward Joseph, a symposium on the identity of the psychoanalyst (*L'Identité du psychanalyste*, Paris: Presses Universitaires de France); John Klauber's contribution to the symposium on that theme formed Chapter 10 of *Difficulties in the Analytic Encounter*.

BIBLIOGRAPHY

The place of publication is London unless indicated otherwise.

Abraham, K. (1924) 'A short study of the development of the libido, viewed in the light of mental disorder', in *Selected Papers of Karl Abraham*. Hogarth, 1949, pp. 418–501.

Adorno, T.W. (1952) 'Zum Verhältnis von Psychoanalyse und Gesellschaftstheorie', *Psyche* 6:1–18.

—— (1955) 'Zum Verhältnis von Soziologie und Psychologie', in R. Tiedemann, ed., *Theodor W. Adorno, Gesammelte Schriften*, vol. 8, *Soziologische Schriften I*. Frankfurt am Main: Suhrkamp, pp. 42–85.

Alexander, F. (1954) 'Some quantitative aspects of psychoanalytic technique', *J. Amer. Psychoanal.* 2:685–701.

—— (1957) 'Development of the theory of psychoanalytic treatment', in *Psychoanalysis and Psychotherapy*. Allen & Unwin, pp. 35–47.

Anzieu, D. (1985) *Le Moi-peau*. Paris: Dunod.

Arlow, J.A. (1979) 'Metaphor and the psychoanalytic situation', *Psychoanal. Q.* 48:363–85.

Ayer, A.J. (1954) 'Freedom and necessity', in Watson, ed. (1982), pp. 15–23.

Balint, A. and Balint, M. (1939) 'On transference and counter-transference'. *Int. J. Psycho-Anal.* 20:223–30.

Balint, M. (1950) 'Changing therapeutic aims and techniques in psycho-analysis', *Int. J. Psycho-Anal.* 31:117–24.

—— (1968) *The Basic Fault: Therapeutic Aspects of Regression.* Tavistock.

Berlin, Isaiah (1979) *Against the Current: Essays in the History of Ideas.* Hogarth.

Bernfeld, S. (1932) 'Der Begriff der "Deutung" in der Psychoanalyse', *Z. Angew. Psychol.* 42:448–97.

Berry, N. (1979) 'Le Roman original', *Nouvelle Revue de Psychanalyse* 26:149–60.

—— (1982) 'La Maison passée présente', *Nouvelle Revue de Psychanalyse* 26:179–93.

—— (1983) 'Portraits de demeures. Un Essai psychanalytique', in *Revue de littérature comparée.* Paris: Didier Littératures.

Bion, W.R. (1962) *Learning from Experience.* Heinemann.

—— (1970) *Attention and Interpretation.* Tavistock.

Bonaparte, M. (1939) *Five Copy Books.* Imago Books, 1950.

Breuer, J. and Freud, S. (1893–5) *Studies on Hysteria*, in James Strachey, ed. *The Standard Edition of the Complete Psychological Works of Sigmund Freud*, 24 vols. Hogarth, 1953–73. vol. 2.

Carveth, D.L. (1984) 'The analyst's metaphors. A deconstructionist perspective', *Psychoanal. Contemp. Thought* 7:491–560.

Casement, P.J. (1973) 'The supervisory viewpoint', in W.F. Finn, ed. *Family Therapy in Social Work: Conference Papers.* Family Welfare Association, pp. 40–5.

—— (1985) *On Learning from the Patient.* Tavistock.

Cecil, David (1929) *The Stricken Deer.* Constable.

Collingwood, R.G. (1938) *The Principles of Art.* Oxford: Clarendon Press.

Copleston, F. (1962) 'St Thomas Aquinas', in *A History of Philosophy*, vol. 2, *Medieval Philosophy, Part II.* New York: Image Books, pp. 94–107.

Dante (1314) *The Divine Comedy. I: Hell*, D. Sayers, trans. Harmondsworth: Penguin, 1949.

Eliot, George (1871–2) *Middlemarch.* Harmondsworth: Penguin, 1965.

Ellenberger, H.F. (1970) *The Discovery of the Unconscious.* Allen & Unwin.

Ezriel, H. (1963) 'Experimentation within the psychoanalytic situation', in L. Paul, ed., *Psychoanalytic Clinical Interpretation*. Free Press of Glencoe, pp. 112–42.

Fairbairn, W.R.D. (1952) *Psychoanalytic Studies of the Personality*. Tavistock.

Favez, G. (1974) 'La Résistance de l'analyse', in *Être psychanalyste*. Paris: Dunod, 1976, pp. 97–104.

Ferenczi, S. (1927) 'The problem of the termination of the analysis', in Ferenczi (1955), pp. 77–86.

—— (1930) 'The principles of relaxation and neocatharsis', in Ferenczi (1955), pp. 108–25.

—— (1955) *Final Contributions to the Problems and Methods of Psycho-Analysis*. Hogarth.

—— (1985) *Journal clinique*. Paris: Payot.

Ferenczi, S. and Rank, O. (1924) *Entwicklungsziele der Psychoanalyse*. Vienna: Int. Psychoanal. Verlag.

Frankfurt, H. (1971) 'Freedom of the will and the concept of a person', in Watson, ed. (1982), pp. 81–95.

Freud, A. (1936) *The Ego and the Mechanisms of Defence*. Hogarth.

Freud, S. (1893) 'On the psychical mechanism of hysterical phenomena: a lecture', in James Strachey, ed. *The Standard Edition of the Complete Psychological Works of Sigmund Freud*, 24 vols. Hogarth, 1953–73. vol. 3, pp. 25–40.

—— (1895) 'Project for a scientific psychology'. S.E. 1, pp. 281–397.

—— (1900) *The Interpretation of Dreams*. S.E. 5.

—— (1905) *Three Essays on the Theory of Sexuality*. S.E. 7, pp. 125–245.

—— (1909) 'Notes upon a case of obsessional neurosis'. S.E. 10, pp. 153–318.

—— (1911) 'Formulations on the two principles of mental functioning'. S.E. 12, pp. 213–26.

—— (1912a) 'The dynamics of transference'. S.E. 12, pp. 97–108.

—— (1912b) 'Recommendations to physicians practising psychoanalysis'. S.E. 12, pp. 109–20.

—— (1913) 'On beginning the treatment'. S.E. 12, pp. 121–44.

—— (1914) 'On narcissism: an introduction'. S.E. 14, pp. 73–102.

—— (1915a) 'Observations on transference love'. S.E. 12, pp. 157–71.

—— (1915b) 'The unconscious'. S.E. 14, pp. 159–215.

—— (1916) 'On transience'. S.E. 14, pp. 303–7.

184 —— (1916–17) *Introductory Lectures on Psychoanalysis*. *S.E.* 15, 16.

—— (1917) 'Mourning and melancholia'. *S.E.* 14, pp. 243–58.

—— (1918) 'From the history of an infantile neurosis'. *S.E.* 17, pp. 1–122.

—— (1919) 'Lines of advance in psychoanalytic therapy'. *S.E.* 17, pp. 157–68.

—— (1923) *The Ego and the Id*. *S.E.* 19, pp. 1–66.

—— (1925) 'An autobiographical study'. *S.E.* 20, pp. 3–74.

—— (1926a) 'Psychoanalysis'. *S.E.* 20, pp. 259–70.

—— (1926b) 'Inhibitions, symptoms and anxiety'. *S.E.* 20, pp. 75–175.

—— (1933) 'The dissection of the psychical personality', *New Introductory Lectures on Psychoanalysis*. *S.E.* 22, pp. 57–80.

—— (1937a) 'Analysis terminable and interminable'. *S.E.* 23, pp. 209–53.

—— (1937b) 'Constructions in analysis'. *S.E.* 23, pp. 255–70.

—— (1940) *An Outline of Psychoanalysis*. *S.E.* 23, pp. 139–207.

—— (1984) 'Ephémère destinée', in *Résultats, idées, problèmes*. Paris: Presses Universitaires de France.

Gaddini, E. (1969) 'On imitation', *Int. J. Psycho-Anal.* 50:475–84.

Gaskill, H.S. (1980) 'The closing phase of the psychoanalytic treatment of adults and the goals of psychoanalysis. "The myth of perfectibility" ', *Int. J. Psycho-Anal.* 61:11–23.

Gill, M.M. (1982) *Analysis of the Transference*. New York: International Universities Press.

Giovacchini, P.L. (1972) 'The blank self', in *Tactics and Techniques in Psychoanalytic Therapy*. New York: Science House, pp. 364–78.

Gitelson, M. (1962) 'The curative factors in psychoanalysis. I: The first phase of psychoanalysis', *Int. J. Psycho-Anal.* 43:194–205.

Gosse, E. (1907) *Father and Son*. Harmondsworth: Penguin, 1949.

Green, A. (1973a) 'Le Genre neutre', in *Narcissisme de vie, narcissisme de mort*. Paris: Minuit, pp. 208–21.

—— (1937b) *Le Discours vivant*. Paris: Presses Universitaires de France.

Greene, Graham (1971) *A Sort of Life*. Harmondsworth: Penguin, 1972.

Greenson, R. (1974) 'Loving, hating and indifference towards the patient', *Int. Rev. Psycho-Anal.* 1:259–66.

Greenson, R., Heimann, P. and Wexler, M. (1970) 'Discussion of the "non-transference relationship in the psychoanalytic situation". Plenary session of the 26th International Psycho-analytical Congress, Rome, 28 July 1969', *Int. J. Psycho-Anal.* 51:143–50.

Grinberg, L. (1980) 'The closing phase of the psychoanalytic treatment of adults and the goals of psychoanalysis', *Int. J. Psycho-Anal.* 61:25–37.

Guntrip, H. (1968) *Schizoid Phenomena: Object Relations and the Self.* Hogarth.

Hampshire, S. (1965) *Freedom of the Individual.* New York: Harper & Row.

Hartmann, H. (1950) 'Comments on the psychoanalytic theory of the ego: introduction', *Psychoanal. Study Child* 5:74–96.

Hartmann, H., Kris, E. and Loewenstein, R.M. (1946) 'Comments on the formation of psychic structure', *Psychoanal. Study Child* 2:11–38.

Hartocollis, P. (1980) 'Time and the dream', *J. Amer. Psychoanal. Assn* 28:861–77.

Heimann, P. (1950) 'On countertransference', *Int. J. Psycho-Anal.* 31:81–4.

—— (1952) *Introjection and Developments in Psycho-Analysis.* Hogarth.

—— (1956) 'Dynamics of transference interpretations', *Int. J. Psycho-Anal.* 37:303–10.

—— (1978) 'Über die Notwendigkeit für den Analytiker mit seinen Patienten natürlich zu sein', in S. Drews *et al.*, eds *Provokation und Toleranz: Alexander Mitscherlich zu ehren – Festschrift für Alexander Mitscherlich zum 70. Geburtstag.* Frankfurt am Main: Suhrkamp, pp. 215–30.

Hoffer, W. (1950) 'Three psychological criteria for the termination of treatment', *Int. J, Psycho-Anal.* 31:194–5.

—— (1952) 'The mutual influences in the development of ego and id: earliest stages', *Psychoanal. Study Child* 7:31–41.

Hume, D. (1740) *A Treatise of Human Nature*, L.A. Selby-Bigge, ed. Oxford: Clarendon Press, 1888.

—— (1751) *An Enquiry Concerning Human Understanding*, P. Nidditch, ed. Oxford: Clarendon Press, 1975.

Hurvich, M. (1970) 'On the concept of reality-testing', *Int. J. Psycho-Anal.* 51:299–312.

186 Jacobson, E. (1964) *The Self and the Object World*. New York: International Universities Press.

James, M. (1960) 'Premature ego development: some observations on disturbances in the first three months of life', *Int. J. Psycho-Anal.* 41:288–94. Reprinted in Kohon, ed. (1986), pp. 101–16.

Jesenská, M. (1985) *Vivre*, C. Ance, trans. Paris: Lieu Commun.

Jung, C.G. (1921) 'The question of the therapeutic value of "abreaction" ', *Br. J. Psychology, Medical Section* 2:13–22.

Kafka, J.S. (1977) 'On reality. An examination of object constancy, ambiguity, paradox and time', *Human Psychiatry* 2:133–58.

Kant, Immanuel (1781) *Critique of Pure Reason*.

—— (1785) *The Moral Law*, H.J. Paton, trans. Hutchinson, 1976.

Kanzer, M. (1979) 'Object relations theory: an introduction', *J. Amer. Psychoanal. Assn* 27:313–25.

Kernberg, O.F. (1975) *Borderline Conditions and Pathological Narcissism*. New York: Jason Aronson.

—— (1979) 'Some implications of object relations theory for psychoanalytic technique', *J. Amer. Psychoanal. Assn* 27 [*Suppl.*]:207–39.

Khan, M.M.R. (1963) 'The concept of cumulative trauma', in *The Privacy of the Self*. Hogarth, 1974, pp. 42–58. Reprinted in Kohon, ed. (1986), pp. 117–35.

Klauber, John (1961) 'The structure of the session as a guide to interpretation', in Klauber (1981), pp. 77–90.

—— (1972) 'On the relationship of transference and interpretation in psychoanalytic therapy'. *Int. J. Psycho-Anal.* 53:385–91. Reprinted in Klauber (1981), pp. 25–43.

—— (1981) *Difficulties in the Analytic Encounter*. New York: Jason Aronson. Reprinted by Free Association Books and Maresfield Library, 1986.

Klein, M. (1950) 'On the criteria for the termination of a psychoanalysis', in *The Writings of Melanie Klein*, vol. 3, *Envy and Gratitude and Other Works 1946–53*, R. Money-Kyrle, ed. Hogarth, 1975, pp. 43–7.

Klein, M., Heimann, P., Isaacs, S. and Rivière, J., eds (1952) *Developments in Psycho-Analysis*. Hogarth.

Kohon, G., ed. (1986) *The British School of Psychoanalysis: The Independent Tradition*. Free Association Books.

Kohut, H. (1971) *The Analysis of the Self*. Hogarth.

—— (1977) *The Restoration of the Self*. New York: International Universities Press.

Kris, Ernst (1956a) 'On some vicissitudes of insight in psychoanalysis', *Int. J. Psycho-Anal.* 37:445–55.

—— (1956b) 'The recovery of childhood memories in psychoanalysis', *Psychoanal. Study Child* 11:254–88.

Lacan, J. (1961) 'Remarque sur le rapport de D. Lagache', *La Psychanalyse* 6. Paris: Presses Universitaires de France.

—— (1966a) 'Le Stade du miroir comme formateur de la fonction du Je', in *Écrits*. Paris: Seuil, pp. 93–100.

—— (1966b) 'L'Aggressivité en psychanalyse', in *Écrits*. Paris: Seuil, pp. 101–24.

Lagache, D. (1961) 'La Psychanalyse et la structure de la personnalité', *La Psychanalyse*. Paris: Presses Universitaires de France, pp. 5–54.

—— (1986) *Oeuvres 8: La Folle de logis. La Psychanalyse comme science exacte*. Paris: Presses Universitaires de France.

Langs, R.J. (1978) *The Listening Process*. New York: Jason Aronson.

Laplanche, J. (1970) *Vie et mort en psychanalyse*. Paris: Flammarion.

Laplanche, J. and Pontalis, J.-B. (1973) *The Language of Psycho-Analysis*. Hogarth.

Loewald, H.W. (1960) 'On the therapeutic action of psychoanalysis', *Int. J. Psycho-Anal.* 41:16–33.

Matte Blanco, I. (1975) *The Unconscious as Infinite Sets*. Duckworth.

Maugham, W. Somerset (1930) *Cakes and Ale*. Harmondsworth: Penguin, 1948.

McDevitt, J.B. (1979) 'The role of internalization in the development of object relations during the separation–individuation phase', *J. Amer. Psychoanal. Assn* 27:327–43.

McLaughlin, J.T. (1981) 'Transference, psychic reality and countertransference', *Psychoanal. Q.* 50:639–64.

Meissner, W.W. (1979) 'Internalization and object relations', *J. Amer. Psychoanal. Assn* 27:345–60.

Mill, J.S. (1859) 'On liberty', in *Utilitarianism*, M. Warnock, ed. Fontana, 1962, pp. 126–50.

Moberly, E.R. (1985) *The Psychology of Self and Other*. Tavistock.

Moss, H. (1963) *The Magic Lantern of Marcel Proust*. Faber & Faber.

188 Nacht, Sacha (1957) 'Technical remarks on the handling of the transference neurosis', *Int. J. Psycho-Anal.* 38:196–203.
—— (1962) 'Curative factors in psychoanalysis', *Int. J. Psycho-Anal.* 43:206–11.
—— (1963) 'The non-verbal relationship in psychoanalytic treatment', *Int. J. Psycho-Anal.* 44:328–33.
—— (1965) 'Criteria and technique for the termination of analysis', *Int. J. Psycho-Anal.* 46:107–16.
Nietzsche, F. (1888) *The Antichrist.* Edinburgh: T.N. Foulis, 1911.
Nouvelle Revue de Psychanalyse (1974) vol. 10: 'Aux limites de l'analysable'.
Nunberg, H. (1932) *Principles of Psychoanalysis.* New York: International Universities Press.
Pascal, B. (1966) *Pensées*, A.J. Krailsheimer, trans. Harmondsworth: Penguin.
Passmore, J. (1957) *A Hundred Years of Philosophy.* Duckworth.
Pontalis, J.-B. (1975) 'Naissance et reconnaisance du "self" ', in *Psychologie de la connaissance de soi.* Paris: Presses Universitaires de France, pp. 271–98.
—— (1977) *Entre le rêve et la douleur.* Paris: Gallimard.
Proust, M. (1926) *A la recherche du temps perdu.* (*Remembrance of Things Past*, vol. 3, *Time Regained.* Terence Kilmartin, trans. Chatto & Windus, 1981.)
Racker, H. (1968) *Transference and Countertransference.* New York: International Universities Press.
Reeves, Joan Wynn (1965) *Thinking about Thinking.* Secker & Warburg.
Richards, A.D. (1980) 'Technical consequences of object relations theory', *J. Amer. Psychoanal. Assn* 28:623–36.
Rosenfeld, H. (1972) 'A critical appreciation of James Strachey's paper on the nature of the therapeutic action of psychoanalysis', *Int. J. Psycho-Anal.* 53:455–61.
Sandler, J. (1976) 'Countertransference and role-responsiveness', *Int. Rev. Psycho-Anal.* 3:43–7.
Sandler, J., Holder, A. and Meers, D. (1963) 'The ego ideal and the ideal self', *Psychoanal. Study Child* 18:139–58.
Schafer, R. (1968) *Aspects of Internalization.* New York: International Universities Press.
Schopenhauer, A. (1841) *Essay on the Freedom of the Will*, K. Kolenda, trans. Indianapolis, IN: Dobbs-Merrill.

Searles, H.F. (1965) *Collected Papers on Schizophrenia and* 189
Related Subjects. New York: International Universities Press.
Segal, H. (1973) *Introduction to the Work of Melanie Klein.*
Revised edn. Hogarth.
Shaw, George Bernard (1905) *Major Barbara.* Bodley Head,
1971.
Spinoza, B. (1678) *Ethics,* R.H.M. Elwes, trans. New York:
Dover Publications, 1955.
Spitz, R.A. (1956) 'Countertransference. Comments on its
varying role in the analytic situation', *J. Amer. Psychoanal.
Assn.* 4:256–65.
Stone, L. (1961) *The Psychoanalytic Situation: An Examin-
ation of its Development and Essential Nature.* New York:
International Universities Press.
Strachey, J. (1934) 'The nature of the therapeutic action of
psycho-analysis', *Int. J. Psycho-Anal.* 15:127–59.
—— (1937) 'On the theory of the therapeutic results of psycho-
analysis', *Int. J. Psycho-Anal.* 18:139–45.
Symington, N. (1986) *The Analytic Experience: Lectures from
the Tavistock.* Free Association Books.
Thomä, H. (1967) *Anorexia Nervosa.* New York: International
Universities Press.
—— (1981) *Schriften zur Praxis der Psychoanalyse: Vom
spiegelnden zum aktiven Psychoanalytiker.* Frankfurt am
Main: Suhrkamp.
Thomä, H. and Kächele, H. (1987) *Psychoanalytic Practice,*
vol. 1, *Principles,* M. Wilson and D. Roseveare, trans. Berlin
and Heidelberg: Springer-Verlag.
Tolstoy, Leo (1903) *Resurrection.* Grant Richard.
Watson, G., ed. (1982) *Free Will.* Oxford: Oxford University
Press.
Watzlawick, P., Beavin, J.H. and Jackson, D.D. (1967) *Prag-
matics of Human Communication. A Study of Interactional
Patterns, Pathologies and Paradoxes.* New York: Norton.
Weinrich, H. (1968) 'Die Metapher', *Poetica* 2:100–30.
Widlöcher, D. (1976) 'Psychoanalysis today: a problem of
identity', in *The Identity of the Psychoanalyst.* New York:
International Universities Press, 1983, pp. 23–39. (First
presented at Haslemere Conference, 1976, and abstracted in
Klauber (1981), pp. 165–9.)
—— (1986) *Métapsychologie du sens.* Paris: Presses Universit-
aires de France.
Winnicott, D.W. (1949) 'Hate in the countertransference', BIBLIOGRAPHY

190   *Int. J. Psycho-Anal.* 30:69–74. Also in Winnicott (1958), pp. 194–203.

—— (1958) *Collected Papers: Through Paediatrics to Psycho-Analysis.* Tavistock.

—— (1965) *The Maturational Processes and the Facilitating Environment.* Hogarth.

—— (1968) 'The use of an object and relating through identifications', in Winnicott (1971a), pp. 101–11.

—— (1971a) *Playing and Reality.* Tavistock.

—— (1971b) 'Note annexe à "Le Corps et le self" ', *Nouvelle Revue de Psychanalyse* 3:35–46.

INDEX

This first edition of
Illusion and Spontaneity
was finished in October 1987.

It was set in 11/14 Sabon
on a Linotron 202 and printed by
a Heidelberg SORS offset press on 80g/m^2 vol. 18 Supreme Antique
Wove.

The book was commissioned by Robert M. Young,
edited and copy-edited by Ann Scott,
designed by Carlos Sapochnik,
indexed by Derek Derbyshire
and produced by David Williams and Selina O'Grady
for Free Association Books.